"I could not put the book down! I could not wait these situations, more importantly, these people and how their lives have been transformed, made this book come alive. I know evangelism. In my work as evangelism specialist for the Tennessee Baptist Convention, I have seen several definitions for the Great Commission work we call evangelism but none as clear and vivid as what I read and saw in the pages of *Faith Acts.*"

—STEVE PEARSON, Harvest Field team leader and evangelism specialist, Tennessee Baptist Convention

"For too long, Christians have embraced the false choice between piety and activism, between gospel proclamation and gospel implications. The gospel of the kingdom, that declares Christ as Lord over all, doesn't allow God's people to live this way. I'm thankful for the winsome call of *Faith Acts*, which issues a necessary challenge to the church toward both courage and civility, to ask what it means to offer the world a glimpse of God's renewal of all things."

—DANIEL DARLING, vice president of communications of The Ethics and Religious Liberty Commission and author of several books including *The Original Jesus*

"Some preach. Some practice. A few do both; they practice what they preach. Jimmy and Dillon are two of those who do both and do it well. Understanding we were all made in the image of God, they reveal their love for God by loving people, especially people who have few to love them. They do what the Bible tells us to do! This book should come with a warning. For as you read it, you too will be compelled to do what it says!"

—DAVID NELMS, president and founder of The Timothy Initiative

"In a world where so many profess faith but turn blind eyes to those in need, stories of action stand out. Showing their personal faith, Jimmy and Dillon share the true meaning of the gospel as they shout without words. All who feel a calling should first read and then find their own 'faith acts.'"

—JENS CHRISTENSEN, chief executive officer of Chattanooga Church Ministries

"*Faith Acts* is a powerful book that challenges you to examine your life, yet helps you demonstrate the love of Jesus toward others. I was very moved after reading this book, and know you will be, too!"

—JASON JIMENEZ, national speaker and cohost of Viral Truth TV

"I am known as a man of action; and therefore, I value action over discussion or passive philosophical bent. Dillon Burroughs and Jimmy Turner are men of action. Men who saw a problem and acted to bring change. Read their book, *Faith Acts*, and then get in the game!"

—CHARLES POWELL, founder of The Mercy Movement

"Unsettling. A little bit disconcerting. Challenging, true, fearless. You can't read this book and remain complacent in your comfortable Christianity. Do you really believe the whole Bible? Not just the parts that settle you but also the parts that unsettle you? I dare you to read this book and go away unchanged."
—JENNIFER KENNEDY DEAN, executive director of The Praying Life Foundation and author of *Live a Praying Life*®, as well as numerous other books and Bible studies

"*Faith Acts: A Provocative Call to Live What You Believe* is one of the most convicting books I've read. Sorry to invoke an old cliché, but literally, 'I could not put it down!' I believe that the authors have created a book that God can use to get countless believers and churches more on track about living out Christ's Great Commission. The true life stories are riveting, and the authors lay out a realistic path for the church to truly engage those who need our help economically and spiritually. In *Faith Acts*, Dillon Burroughs and Jimmy Turner stir the heart and motivate the soul! Their ability to communicate truth through riveting stories and true life accounts makes this book a perfect read for the times in which we live. I highly recommend it."
—ALEX MCFARLAND, director of the Center for Christian Worldview and Apologetics, North Greenville University

FAITH ACTS

A PROVOCATIVE CALL
TO LIVE WHAT
YOU BELIEVE

DILLON BURROUGHS
—— AND ——
JIMMY TURNER

To my favorite
shelter manager,
Kathy - Keep
doing good!!

Dillon Burroughs

Romans
5:8

NEW HOPE®
PUBLISHERS
Gospel-Centered. Missions-Driven.

BIRMINGHAM, ALABAMA

New Hope® Publishers
PO Box 12065
Birmingham, AL 35202-2065
NewHopePublishers.com
New Hope Publishers is a division of WMU®.

New Hope Publishers serves its authors as they express their views, which may
not express the views of the publisher.

Names have been changed to protect the identities of individuals mentioned in
this book.

Library of Congress Cataloging-in-Publication Data

Names: Burroughs, Dillon.
Title: Faith acts : a provocative call to live what you believe / Dillon
   Burroughs and Jimmy Turner.
Description: Birmingham, AL : New Hope Publishers, 2016.
Identifiers: LCCN 2015039897 | ISBN 9781596694675 (sc)
Subjects: LCSH: Church work with the homeless--Tennessee--Chattanooga Region.
Classification: LCC BV4456 .B865 2016 | DDC 253--dc23 LC record available at
http://lccn.loc.gov/2015039897

ISBN-10: 1-59669-467-X
ISBN-13: 978-1-59669-467-5

N164107 • 0316 • 2M1

Dedicated to the homeless men, women,

and children of Tennessee.

———

Other New Hope books
by DILLON BURROUGHS

Hunger No More

Thirst No More

Not in My Town
(with Charles Powell)

CONTENTS

FOREWORD BY JEFF FOXWORTHY 9

ACKNOWLEDGMENTS 11

INTRODUCTION. 13
Why *Faith Acts* Matter
JIMMY TURNER

CHAPTER 1 17
Do You Really Believe the Bible?
Pretest on Faith and Action
JIMMY TURNER

CHAPTER 2 27
A Kingdom Not of This World
Faith + Politics – Hatred = Impact
DILLON BURROUGHS

CHAPTER 3 45
Taking Scripture Seriously
You Mean You Really Believe This Stuff?
JIMMY TURNER

CHAPTER 4 57
Tag, You're Called
For Many Issues, You Already Know God's Will
DILLON BURROUGHS

CHAPTER 5 73
Following the Great Commission
and the Great Commandment
Jesus Didn't Say, "Choose One of the Above"
JIMMY TURNER

CHAPTER 6 89
Ctrl + Alt + Del Church
A Fresh Look at Church in Action
DILLON BURROUGHS

CHAPTER 7 105
Controversies 'R Us
When Taking a Stand Means Taking a Hit
DILLON BURROUGHS

CHAPTER 8 121
Together We Can
Applying Scripture Is a Team Sport
JIMMY TURNER

A FINAL WORD 137

DISCUSSION GUIDE 145

**APPENDIX: MINISTERING
TO INDIVIDUALS WITH PTSD** 153

**FREQUENTLY ASKED QUESTIONS
ABOUT RELEVANT HOPE** 159

ABOUT RELEVANT HOPE 169

ABOUT THE AUTHORS 171

FOREWORD

There is a tremendous difference between talking a good talk and living it. To "do what it says," as the Bible challenges, requires a high level of commitment.

In this culture that often displays apathy toward those in need, Dillon Burroughs and Jimmy Turner stand as unique examples and powerful ambassadors of a different way. Their book, *Faith Acts,* provides a roadmap that clearly demonstrates living out kindness includes showing love to those in the most difficult situations.

Burroughs and Turner offer living proof that small acts of kindness performed with great love transforms the addict, the disabled, the poor, and the despised. "Do what it says" serves as both a command and way of life.

To read the stories of men and women changed through simple acts of compassion serves as an inspiration to those of us who long to see change among the less fortunate living on the streets of our communities. Despite persecution, misunderstanding, and messy situations, their actions show that taking a risk is the best way to bring light to those walking in darkness.

In *Faith Acts,* Burroughs and Turner chronicle their journey in an exciting, adventurous, and inspiring way. It is a saga that will motivate readers toward a renewed commitment to "being the change" where they live. It will also convict you to rise up from your struggles and move forward to serve others, no matter the cost. You will discover that the blessing of helping others changes our own lives as well, something I regularly experience in my efforts to assist the poor and homeless of my own community.

We dare not shrink from the many problems in our society. We each have a role to play to make a difference where we live. Burroughs and Turner show the cost may be high, but the battle is worth it, and the people whose lives are changed are definitely worth the effort.

Regardless of where you stand in your journey, this book is for you. These pages will remind you we are not the spectators in life; we are the players who are called to give our best efforts on the field with the abilities we have been given. Join those who are living out what it means to love your neighbor as yourself, no matter where the journey leads.

Jeff Foxworthy

COMEDIAN, TV HOST,

AND BESTSELLING AUTHOR

ACKNOWLEDGMENTS

The cover of this book includes two names, but many people contributed to the story. Our friends, volunteers, donors, staff, and board members of Relevant Hope are each part of bringing the principles of this book alive in our community.

In particular, we want to acknowledge the friendship and support of the following individuals, couples, and organizations:

Martin and Debbie Pierce

Continuon Services LLC

Tim and Pepper Wilson

The Timothy Initiative

Saint Alexius Outreach Ministries

Welcome Home of Chattanooga

Met-Min (Metropolitan Ministries)

Marc and Cayla Wilson

Lindsey Brown and family

Bill and Lisa Turner (Turner Security)

Jens and the staff of the Chattanooga Community Kitchen who work closely with us to serve our outside neighbors

Recognition in memory and honor of Otis and Martha Walker

The Meeting House

Adam and Stephanie Whitescarver

Chattanooga House of Prayer

In addition, our family members have greatly influenced our lives each day of the journey.

FROM DILLON: Thank you to my wife, Deborah, for an amazing 17 years of marriage! You are my best friend and greatest partner in serving God. To my children, Ben, Natalie, and Audrey, I love each of you and pray our heavenly Father continues to offer me opportunities to enjoy every moment possible with you.

FROM JIMMY: Thank you to my wife, Shay, for your faithful, caring, and loving partnership throughout our journey. To my sons, A. J. and Taylor, you are gifts from God I treasure dearly. I look forward to many more years of being Dad to two of most amazing young men on the planet.

In addition, our friends at New Hope have worked hard to improve our efforts to communicate God's story to others. Thank you to Judy Patterson, Joyce Dinkins, Melissa Hall, Mark Bethea, Reagan Jackson, and Kathy Caltabelotta. We also thank Andrea Mullins for her leadership as previous publisher at New Hope and her support in our writing ministry.

As we have repeated from our founding, together we can. We can and are changing lives now and for eternity through a growing, committed team of family and friends who believe the best way to show God's love is through how we treat the most vulnerable people in our community.

Finally, we foremost thank our God and Savior Jesus Christ, who has considered us trustworthy, appointing us to His service (1 Timothy 1:12). To Him be the glory.

INTRODUCTION

WHY *FAITH ACTS* MATTER

———— JIMMY TURNER ————

August 2013: Today I'm in a lake baptizing a man named Tree. We met under a bridge a few weeks ago, and what was unthinkable just days before is now happening before my eyes. A man who had lived on the streets for more than a decade was being transformed for eternity.

I am not that much different from you. After a few years as a marine, I returned to the States to work in law enforcement and then started college. During those years, I sensed God calling me to serve Him in ministry. As I neared graduation, I began to realize "ministry" for me would not take the form of a pastor in a building with a steeple or wearing a suit and tie. Instead, my heart was being changed to pursue a missions field untouched in my community—those living with no address and no home.

In Chattanooga, Tennessee, there are more than 1,000 churches. If anyone is interested in hearing from God, they can probably find a service any night of the week and even live on communion wafers and juice for food, but that doesn't mean everyone in town is a Christian. In fact, many feel unwelcome in traditional churches, especially the homeless. Think about it—how would your church respond if a handful of homeless men and women showed up for church Sunday morning?

These invisible people dot the landscape of our downtown and surrounding regions, typically unknown and unloved. Panhandling is illegal in many parts of our town, and parks where the homeless once stayed are closed after dark. Many tent cities have also been destroyed over the years to communicate such people must "move on."

Don't misunderstand; there are several noble local service providers. But for whatever reason, only about half of the homeless in our community utilize such services. The story of the lost sheep in Luke 15 comes to mind—who is willing to leave the 99 to pursue the one?

Dillon and I first met when he was the professor of my apologetics class during my last semester of college. As we discussed future plans and community needs, it became clear we both had a heart for those in our community who live outside. By the time the semester ended, we decided to start with checking out local sites where homeless people had been reported as staying and try to connect with them.

After a few failed attempts at abandoned homeless camps, we visited under a bridge near downtown where we met a guy who called himself Tree. It was about eight in the morning, yet he was delighted to have some company. We introduced ourselves, shared what we had in mind, and asked if it was OK to come back with some breakfast and meet again. He invited us to return and then mentioned another nearby location where some people were staying outside.

Following Tree's lead, we walked to the next location. Entering an uncharted tree line near a polluted creek, Dillon and I pushed aside brush and called out, "Good morning." We were met by two men—Sky and Chris—and one woman named Paula who happened to carry a machete.

We were unsure what to expect. Would they turn violent? All I could do was pray and keep calm. After introducing ourselves, Paula opened up and began talking vibrantly about their outdoor life. Among the beer cans and debris, God began to open discussions about life, family, and how we could become friends.

Before we left, Dillon asked if it was OK to pray together. We did, followed by hugs from everyone before leaving. Two thoughts struck me: First, these homeless people were friendlier than many Christians I had met. Second, I wondered how long it had been since these people had received a caring hug and friendship from another person. Our search ended with the start of Relevant Hope—our mission to serve the homeless wherever they are and provide whatever they need.

Since then, much has changed. Dillon and I officially founded Relevant Hope to serve the homeless in our community. In the first year, we began more than a dozen outdoor churches in partnership with the Tennessee Baptist Convention's 1-5-1 Harvest Program. As executive director of Relevant Hope, I initially led our many scattered congregations, and then later recruited and trained others for these roles. Instead of visiting for hours in one camp, this outreach now visits more than 60 locations just in our local area. I have since moved on from my role with Relevant Hope, and today Dillon serves as the executive director.

Interest has increased beyond our area as well. New movements are under discussion throughout Tennessee for similar groups. Church leaders have visited from across the nation to see what "faith in action" looks like among the homeless of a community.

Looking back, I tell people that it all began with deciding to not only read the Word, but to "do what it says" (James 1:22). When I think of success, I don't focus on numbers or donations; I think back to the day Tree decided to believe in Jesus. His baptism was the beginning of a new life. Today, he lives inside—he has a permanent place to call home—and helps us in the efforts to reach others through Relevant Hope. There was no class in college for this type of work. Instead, this training is straight from God's Word. We are called to do what it says.

CHAPTER 1

DO YOU REALLY BELIEVE THE BIBLE?

PRETEST ON FAITH AND ACTION

JIMMY TURNER

Let's begin with a quick survey: First, have you read the Bible on your own in the last seven days (not including at a church service)? Second, do you believe the Bible is accurate in what it teaches?

How did you do? If you replied yes to both questions, you are considered a Bible-minded person according to the criteria of a recent Barna survey. My hometown of Chattanooga was ranked the "most Bible-minded city" in 2014 based on these criteria. In addition, 64 percent of Chattanooga's residents reportedly attend church on a weekly basis. This percentage of church attendance is the largest in the 100 major metropolitan areas included in the study. The Greater Chattanooga area hosts more than 1,000 churches. There is space for anyone interested in going to church in this city, with room to spare.

Chattanooga's vast number of churches and the data presented by Barna, who worked jointly with the American Bible Society to record this information, would give anyone confidence in the cultural impact of the Bible on Chattanooga. After all, how could more than 60 percent of the community's population read the Bible on a regular basis but not impact those around them? They read it and believe it. Shouldn't we be confident they also regularly apply it? The expectation would be for the community to break out in revival and change societal problems at a significant level. Yet a closer look reveals a deep disconnect between surveys of "Bible-mindedness" and Bible application. There is tremendous difference between awareness and action.

Chattanooga's crime and poverty statistics communicate another story. In 2013, the city recorded 19 homicides. By July 2014, Chattanooga had already passed the previous year's total with a twentieth homicide. Worse, over the past three years, half of these murder cases have remained unresolved. While city and law enforcement leaders are launching new initiatives to change these statistics, the situation does not reflect a community changed by God's Word. In fact, the state of Tennessee, in which Chattanooga is the fourth-largest city, recently ranked number one in the nation for violent crime.

Chattanooga's homeless population is as tragic as its crime. Chattanooga has 635 people on any given night without a permanent residence. More than 4,000 individuals will experience homelessness at least one night in Chattanooga during the year; approximately one-fourth of these people are children. With only one permanent emergency shelter that holds less than 100 people, Chattanooga's homeless population must take to the streets for a bed. Some are able to find shelter through the limited programs available, but close to 200 people a night will sleep unsheltered regardless of the weather. Chattanooga once put in place a plan to end chronic homelessness over a ten-year period, but nearly ten years later, the numbers are just as high or higher than when the initiative began.

A tremendous void stands between what the people of Chatta-nooga say they believe and the application of these beliefs to the needs of society. Barna's standard for being Bible-minded (read-ing your Bible and believing in its accuracy) is the very thing the Bible warns can *deceive* us. James wrote, "Do not merely listen to the word, and *so deceive yourselves.* Do what it says" (James 1:22, author's emphasis). James further taught that faith without works is dead (2:26). If the most Bible-minded city in the United States is facing increasing levels of homelessness and homicides, it's not because believers are in the streets living out their faith. It's due to knowing what the Bible says yet being content to live aware without application. Reading the Bible is a great starting point, but it is not the end point.

I think we would all agree that unaddressed crime and pov-erty are in direct conflict with the Bible's principles. Those who are in Christ are new creations, and their criminal lives will be left behind. Jesus said if we love Him, we would obey Him. How did He tell us to live? He said that the Great Commandment is to love God and love our neighbor. Are we loving our neighbor when we refuse to help a person on the street? Are we loving our neighbor when we seek to make homelessness a crime (as many cities now have)? Are we living the way of Jesus when we move out of town to avoid problems instead of leaving the comfort of home to serve those in need?

Are we willing to put our lives on the line in the United States of America, in our hometowns, and for the sake of the gospel? We expect missionaries overseas to put their lives on the line. We even donate the resources to help because we tell ourselves the missions field is "over there." The reality for America, however, is that the missions field is next door, the next person we meet, the next street, and the next store. Instead of engaging people to share Christ, we often judge them, condemn them, and even flee from them.

Churches are friends, connections of people who hold one common bond—the Son of God—whose blood was poured out for the doubters and despised, poor and wise. Jesus communicated these things when He read a portion from the prophet Isaiah:

> *The Spirit of the LORD is upon me, for he has anointed me to bring Good News to the poor. He has sent me to proclaim that captives will be released, that the blind will see, that the oppressed will be set free, and that the time of the LORD's favor has come.*
>
> —LUKE 4:18–19 NLT

Good news to the poor, the captives, the blind, and the oppressed. The time of the Lord's favor has come. Jesus has come. He leaves us to be Jesus to those still oppressed and confused.

The church—you, me, and everybody who claims the name of Jesus. So stop complaining about all the hypocrites. Be the church that speaks love, truth, compassion, and grace to those living without purpose and without hope.

> Homeless church.
> Where you and I can both be members because of one homeless man who took our place and gave us grace.
> *Jesus.*
>
> —Dillon Burroughs, from *Undefending Christianity*

ARE YOU A FRIEND OF SINNERS?

When I got out of the Marine Corps, I wasn't sure what kind of work I would do. I was an expert marksman, but that doesn't help much in finding a civilian job. I wasn't used to feeling hopeless, but that is exactly how I felt. I had no idea what I was going to do to provide for my wife and two sons.

Someone recommended that I should apply to work at one of our local prisons. The salary was decent, and the work sounded fun, so I applied. After starting the job, I didn't have to work long before I realized I was meshed with a variety of people I would not normally otherwise encounter. I was shocked to learn some of the inmates I supervised were well-educated, white-collar individuals from the suburbs. I also learned some of the people around me were convicted murderers, bank robbers, and drug dealers. I knew going into the job I would encounter criminals, but I didn't realize how serious it was until I had the opportunity to learn firsthand about the people around me.

In addition to the diverse group of inmates, I was also surrounded with much variety in my co-workers. Some of my co-workers were everyday people simply working to pay the bills. Others were well educated, with a desire to further their careers in criminal justice or law enforcement. In addition, a few co-workers could barely make it through a shift without taking a drink. One guy was actually fired because he would take a break and grab a few drinks from his car. Other co-workers were sexually promiscuous or were in same-sex relationships.

During my time working at the jail, I was not a professing Christian. At that time, I considered myself agnostic and apathetic. I didn't care if there was a God or whether I could know Him. I was familiar with Christianity and grew up in a culturally Christian home. As a kid, I walked an aisle (several times) and was baptized on multiple occasions to make sure I would go to heaven, as I was often told I had lost my salvation because I didn't fit the Christian culture around me. By adulthood, I considered most Christians judgmental hypocrites who seemed to take pleasure from condemning people to hell. I was happy not to associate myself with them.

During this time at the prison, God began to work in my life. I didn't know why I was starting to have questions about religion and spiritual issues, but I felt a desire to know what was true. God was drawing me, Jesus was interrupting my life, and I was on my way to a Damascus Road-like change that would transform my efforts from making a living to making a difference.

I don't know the exact day or hour Christ saved me, but I know it happened because I was a changed person. I didn't realize I was different, but when my wife commented I had changed, I knew I was a new creation. I wasn't sure how I was supposed to act or what church I was supposed to attend, so I simply started by reading the Bible. I found a Bible app for my phone with a 90-day reading plan to get me through the entire Bible. One thing I realized from my quick read through Scripture was that Christians were to live in community with other believers. That calling meant I needed to find a church family.

Reading Scripture also showed me God wants us to reach people outside our circle of church friends. I wanted desperately to be like Jesus. I wanted to be a friend to sinners. Today, I am pleased to say I have many friends in my life who aren't Christians. I don't misuse our friendship as an opportunity to condemn them, but I talk with them about spiritual topics and God because I am their friend. Some have put faith in Jesus because the Holy Spirit has worked through our friendship to save them. Others are asking questions and taking the time to learn what it means to fall short of God's glory. Some still appear to be as distant from God as when I first met them. You never know how God will change someone's life, but you'll also never find out unless you try.

WOULD YOU BE CONVICTED IF IT WAS A CRIME TO BE A CHRISTIAN?

In many nations, you can be arrested or even face death for being a Christian. I know. From serving in the Middle East as a marine, I've seen how some cultures show little or no mercy for those who accept a religion different from their own. While America prides itself for religious freedom, other nations often pride themselves for allowing only one religion or worldview, forcing everyone to conform or otherwise face punishment.

But what if the rules changed and being a Christian in our own nation was a crime? How easily would you be convicted for being a Christian? Though our salvation is based on faith, not works, James was clear that faith without works is dead. Jesus also said our actions should allow others to see our good deeds and draw them to give glory to our Father in heaven (Matthew 5:16).

What evidence would be used to convict you? A fish bumper sticker or Christian T-shirt is not enough. In other nations that persecute believers, the reasons usually include claiming Jesus is the only God (John 14:6; Acts 4:12), maintaining close connections with other Christians, receiving baptism, openly praying to God, reading the Bible, and starting efforts to share faith and serve others.

My tendency is to hope for the best in people when working among the homeless. In other words, I believe their claims until I have a reason to doubt. When we met Darren under a bridge, he told us he was new to the area and just needed to get by until his parents could come and pick him up. He was around 30 years old and admitted to being a serious alcoholic.

Then he told us that he couldn't quit drinking because he was afraid of dying during the detox period. He shared that a few weeks earlier, he was staying in a hotel room with a friend who was trying to detox. Darren claimed his friend's body couldn't take the detox, and his friend died. Darren called 911 while he was attempting CPR to keep him alive, but it didn't help. Because of this experience, Darren was terrified of being arrested because he knew that if he went to jail, he would be forced to detox without medication. He cried to us for half an hour about wanting to stop drinking but not without a medical detox program.

I set up an appointment for Darren to see a case manager who could give him a referral for a state-run rehab facility that would medically detox him from alcohol. I returned under the bridge where Darren was staying to tell him the good news, and he expressed genuine excitement. When the day came for Darren's appointment, I went to his camp to give him a ride. I had reminded him the day before that he had to be sober when he went to the appointment. He had promised to quit drinking before midnight to make sure he could make it.

When I arrived at his camp, I woke him and let him know I was ready to take him to the appointment. He mumbled something and rolled away from me. I tried waking him again and reminded him about his appointment. He sat up and said, "Didn't think that was a good idea." When I asked him why, he pulled a bottle of vodka out from under his sleeping bag and took a big drink.

I felt betrayed. I wondered how he could just take another drink after all the effort I made to help him change. Darren had been telling me he wanted something different, but his lifestyle told me another story. His words were saying that he wanted to be sober and productive in life, but his actions were telling me he was not serious about change.

Darren's story is tragic, but it is the story of many believers as well. We can claim to be a Christian, wear the right clothes, use the right language, or attend a Bible study, but is our lifestyle providing a different testimony? If an outside auditor analyzed our lives—how we use our time, how we spend money, how we treat others—would there be sufficient evidence we were devoted followers of Christ? Christianity is more than a label; it is a radically different lifestyle.

HOW DID YOU SCORE?

We've discussed three key issues related to how much we really believe the Bible. First, how clearly is your faith working in action? Second, can you be accused of being a friend of sinners? Third, is there sufficient evidence to convict you of being a devoted follower of Christ? If you're like us, you'll find both a mix of strengths and weaknesses in these areas. We're all works in progress, but the key is to continue moving forward. In our next chapter, we'll discover how our view of the Bible influences the way we study it and live it out each day. Stay with us, as we're in for a journey with the potential to change your life and the lives of many others.

A KINGDOM NOT OF THIS WORLD

FAITH + POLITICS - HATRED = IMPACT

DILLON BURROUGHS

'*ve never slept on the streets . . . but I've been close.

In 2005, my family and I moved back to the Indianapolis area after six years in Texas. I found a job and worked out an arrangement for my family of four to stay at my brother-in-law's home until we found a new place. Four months later, my job abruptly ended.

I had no income and nowhere to turn.

What began as "a few weeks with family" became a one-year rewrite of my life. I often worked from before six in the morning until six in the evening or later, first looking for a job, and then working one or more jobs at a time. By the end of a year, we were able to rent a new place and stand on our own again.

My goal now is to do all I can to help others in similar situations. My brother-in-law didn't have to let us stay, but he did. Many people lack family or friends with such resources. They don't have a back-up plan when life comes crashing down.

My position as executive director of Relevant Hope allows me to help people in a variety of situations ranging from the chronic homeless to those staying in a hotel room or in a car who don't know where they'll sleep the next night.

Every story is different, but one thing remains the same—everybody needs hope. As long as I'm alive, I will be a hope to those in need.

LET'S GET POLITICAL

Outsiders unfortunately see evangelicals, political conservatives, and extremists who want to overthrow the government all as members of the same religious freak show—people to be avoided at all costs. At the same time, spirituality is increasingly accepted as an important part of culture. A major part of my work is helping people who call themselves "spiritual but not religious" see that the true, biblical Jesus is only one who will satisfy their longing for a spiritual relationship based on unconditional love. It's basically Ephesians 4:15, "speaking the truth in love."

On the other extreme, many conservative, Bible-believing Christians are overwhelmed by culture and are not sure what to do, sometimes calling all cultural changes bad. Jesus was a friend to sinners and lived among ordinary people, yet He continued to teach and live the truth. That balance is the dynamic I seek to live and promote, learning all I can and communicating it to others along the way.

Forging this path is not easy. Christians claim to care about the poor, yet when challenged to become more involved in local community efforts to change the situation, few are willing to step forward. The church is called to serve those in need. Local, state, and national governments exist to meet certain societal needs as well. In some cases, there are ways to participate that can serve what is called the common good. We need not fear these types of relationships but rather should work carefully both to honor God and to show love to those in need.

For example, in the early days of Relevant Hope, a homeless camp was bulldozed without warning, leaving many people displaced. While we understand the residents were there without permission, the city and the company involved in the demolition could have handled the situation far better. Jimmy took action that consisted first in helping those on the street and then contacting our local city offices. In the end, he convinced law enforcement to call us the next time a homeless person needed to move to a different location.

And they have. Since this incident, our city and community leaders increasingly reach out to let us know of situations where homeless individuals are about to be displaced from a location. When this happens, we do all we can to help these people move to a new location or find housing. In some cases, we even help clean up the mess left behind after they move. We call it our "good neighbor" policy.

Could you imagine a community where the homeless are not simply pushed aside or arrested but are lovingly assisted in moving to another location, connected with resources, and encouraged to pursue options that lead toward jobs and housing? This transformation only happens when we pursue the common good rather than the good of any one organization.

GO AND DO LIKEWISE

The attitude to "go and do likewise" is not only practical, it's biblical. In the account of the Good Samaritan, Jesus taught that it was not the religious elite who were the most loving people but those who showed their love for God through helping those most in need. In fact, the person who stopped to help the injured man was a Samaritan, an ethnic group despised by most Jews. Jesus said:

But a Samaritan, as he traveled, came where the man was; and when he saw him, he took pity on him. He went to him and bandaged his wounds, pouring on oil and wine. Then he put the man on his own donkey, brought him to an inn and took care of him. The next day he took out two denarii and gave them to the inn-keeper. "Look after him," he said, "and when I return, I will reimburse you for any extra expense you may have."

—LUKE 10:33-35

First, he had compassion for someone in need. The Greek word trans-lated "he took pity" is the same word often translated as "he had compassion." The first two men who passed apparently lacked compassion for the man. They were more concerned about other matters.

Second, he went to the person in need. The Levite and priest would have likely been more responsive if the injured man had come over to them and asked for help, but he couldn't. It required a person will-ing to change his normal course of action to act with compassion. Much of our success with Relevant Hope has come from our strong focus on going to those in need rather than expecting them to figure out where to go for help.

Third, he chose to help. Compassion without action is meaning-less. We can feel badly for someone, but that doesn't help unless we are willing to stop and do something. I've wanted to help the poor since I became a Christian, yet I have often neglected to act on this desire. Why? There are always reasons—some valid, some not—but in the end, inaction equals apathy. I simply did not care enough to do anything but keep walking. In the Samaritan's case, he treated the man's wounds, took him to an inn, and covered his expenses. Many observations can be made from the Samaritan's actions.

Fourth, he offered unconditional service. The Samaritan did not stop to ask whether the hurt man was a Jew or Samaritan or whether he was Democrat or Republican. He saw a person in need and stopped.

Fifth, he served beyond expectations. Under normal circumstances, a person might expect someone to stop and help, making sure the man could get up and walk on his own, yet the Samaritan took the man to an inn on his own donkey. He used his own transportation to take the man in need to the ancient equivalent of a hotel and paid for the room until he was well enough to leave.

I often think of this aspect of the Good Samaritan account when we provide emergency housing for people. We are unable to afford housing for every person we help, but on some occasions, it's simply the right thing to do. When it is five degrees outside and a person only has a coat and backpack, a Good Samaritan gets that person indoors.

I also often think of this account in another area of life—transporting homeless people around town. When we first began direct service to the homeless in our community, I didn't expect to drive people from underpasses to hospitals or hotel rooms. The first time I gave some of our homeless friends a ride, I had to move my daughter's car seat quickly to make room. It was at this point that I knew I was on the right track. My concern for helping those in need was greater than my desire to keep my van clean or organized. Today, the back of my van usually looks like that of a disaster-relief vehicle. I carry food, clothes, blankets, Bibles, tarps, and other supplies to help people along the way. Carrying these items would have never crossed my mind when we bought the vehicle that has now become a vital part of serving those in need in our community.

When Jesus finished His story, He asked,

> *"Which of these three do you think was a neighbor to the man who fell into the hands of robbers?" The expert in the law replied, "The one who had mercy on him." Jesus told him, "Go and do likewise."*
>
> —LUKE 10:36–37

These words need no explanation, only application. Go and do likewise.

EXTENDING THE VISION

Paul's second missions trip was far different than his first. He had new co-workers and even struggled with which direction to take. Then Acts 16:9–10 reveals,

> *During the night Paul had a vision of a man of Macedonia standing and begging him, "Come over to Macedonia and help us." After Paul had seen the vision, we got ready at once to leave for Macedonia, concluding that God had called us to preach the gospel to them.*

As Paul continued his efforts to share the good news, the Lord increased his vision.

God often operates in this way still today. I remember when we were about a year into Relevant Hope. So much was happening that we could barely keep up, and yet there was a burden I could not shake. Through many prayers and various confirmations, I sensed God wanted Relevant Hope eventually to reach beyond Chattanooga to serve other places in our state. With a little research, we found that about one in four of Tennessee's nearly 10,000 homeless people on any given day are in the greater Nashville area. Jimmy and I prayed and sought God's guidance on where to begin.

We chose one morning to take a visit to Nashville to see who we could meet. Our first stop was at a location that held a weekly outreach for the homeless. We found no homeless individuals in this neighborhood and decided to stop by the local rescue mission to introduce ourselves and seek some guidance.

Our visit proved to be God's providence in action. We met an outreach worker who talked with us about his work and mentioned several locations of Nashville's homeless. We decided to try a wooded area nearby first, hoping to find an encampment similar to what we usually served in our community.

We prayed we would find one or two people. Instead, we met several individuals who invited us to visit with them and talk. We learned much about their needs and personal stories, which prompted possible ways we could help.

I wish we could say we have since transformed the city, but this vision is still a work in progress. As I look at Paul's initial efforts after his vision of Macedonia, I find comfort that we are not alone. Immediately following his vision, his team traveled to Philippi, a Roman outpost where only a few Jews lived. Paul and his friends "went outside the city gate to the river, where we expected to find a place of prayer" (Acts 16:13) on the Sabbath day. A woman named Lydia and her household believed that day and invited Paul and his friends to stay at their home. Though Paul and Silas would soon face prison and be forced to leave this city, Philippi became a vibrant church Paul would write to years later, saying, "I thank my God every time I remember you" (Philippians 1:3).

Similarly, as God allows us to extend our efforts beyond our local area, we carefully seek to pursue His plan to serve others. Our goal is to meet needs, build friendships, and leave an impact in the lives of many others through our love for Jesus.

ONE CHURCH, ONE CITY, ONE MISSION

I've often presented the challenge for a local church to provide a location for homeless residents to camp on church property. I never personally witnessed this bold expression of love in action until our first visit with Relevant Hope in Nashville.

The church's name, Green Street Church of Christ, is not as trendy as those of some of the emerging congregations that dot the downtown landscape, yet their focus has attracted both local and national notoriety. While ministering to the homeless near their church, they offered the opportunity to set up camp on their own property. One tent became two until more than a dozen tents covered the church's yard.

When adjacent businesses began to complain, the church invested in a privacy fence around the area and began to enforce a few basic rules to avoid problems among those who camped. Volunteers provide daily meals, friendship, and other services while assisting each person with his or her next step toward employment and housing. Even if a small fraction of the city's churches took such a courageous approach, homelessness would virtually disappear in one of America's largest cities.

When I asked one of the volunteers why he helped there, he told me he had once been homeless and just wanted to help. He understood the issues of those living on the street and wanted to help others on their journey toward recovery. Devoting his time, some basic cooking, and a desire to help, he and other members of Green Street are quietly igniting a revolution we hope to encourage nationwide.

NAME THAT CHURCH

Many people and even churches want to help the poor and homeless of their community, but they don't know how to care for their local homeless while also serving the needs of current members. I encourage churches to become known as the place where the poor and homeless can go to find help. If I came to your town and asked any person on the street, "Which church should I go to if I want to get involved in helping the poor or homeless in this community?" would your church be the first one mentioned? Make this identity your goal.

Of course, this identity is not easy. If it was, every church would do it. In fact, you'll likely get in trouble along the way. In some cities, you must now obtain a permit simply to feed the homeless. Green Street has faced numerous complaints from businesses and even other Christians who feel their approach is inappropriate.

Our goal is not to make everybody happy by how we help the poor or even to feel good about our work or ourselves. In the end, are the poor being helped? Are the hungry being fed? Are the homeless being housed? Are those who need clothing being clothed? Are the thirsty receiving water? Are the sick receiving medical care? Are those imprisoned being visited? Are those held in bondage being freed? We want to care most about what Jesus cares most about.

ENDING SLAVERY, ONE LIFE AT A TIME

Speaking of bondage, do you realize that slavery still exists? There are an estimated 30 million slaves worldwide, more than the total number of slaves that existed during the transatlantic slave trade. In my work to fight human trafficking (the more modern term for slavery), I met with Mercy Movement founder Charles Powell to discuss how close to home this issue persists. We met in a café in the northwest suburbs of Atlanta and found a case of forced slave labor at a restaurant only minutes away. Most people in the café where we were sitting likely had no idea these crimes had taken place in their own community.

Likewise, when I researched sex trafficking situations near my office, I realized there had been incidents reported within walking distance. In fact, in a recent two-year period, our state of Tennessee has reported sex trafficking cases in 85 percent of its counties. But what can be done? What is being done? How can we be a part of the solution?

My goal has been simple: research, report, and reduce. I've worked hard to discover any trafficking situations in my area, report them, and do all I can to speak out to help prevent and reduce the number of people who live in bondage. In fact, my work with Relevant Hope sometimes crosses over into the area of advocacy for sex trafficking victims. It's not uncommon to find people on the street who have sold themselves or have been sold for sexual services in the past. We also occasionally find men who have used such services on the streets. Through helping people in both situations find new hope and life, local incidents are being greatly reduced. Even if one person's life is spared from slavery as a result, all of our efforts will have been worth it.

WORKING SMALL, DREAMING BIG

The King James Version of Proverbs 29:18 says, "Where there is no vision, the people perish," and yet we've also found that without a parish—a community of believers—there is no vision. In other words, as we work together as a team, God grows our dreams into something greater than we can accomplish alone.

When we talk about the future of Relevant Hope, we remember the first person we met under a bridge, yet we dream of a day when our efforts influence thousands across our state and beyond. In the days ahead, we are committed to the following vision.

First, we will seek to impact the homeless in our community at a more personal level. With more than 600 homeless individuals in our area on any given day, we must improve our systems, increase the number of trained volunteers, and build greater alliances with churches and community groups to show dignity and care to every person.

Second, we will pursue ways to serve the nearly 10,000 homeless of our state of Tennessee. We realize we will never reach every single homeless individual within our state's borders, but we can and will pursue ways to serve as many people as possible, beginning with our efforts in Nashville and extending to other major cities across the state.

Third, we will pursue national and international partnerships to improve the lives of the homeless. We have already discovered more than 100 similar organizations nationwide that serve the homeless locally. We want both to better connect with such groups and to help multiply similar ministries in every place.

Fourth, we desire to serve alongside our brothers and sisters in Christ worldwide who serve the poor and homeless by providing relevant needs and future hope. Only together can we encourage, equip, and empower on a global scale to truly serve as the hands and feet of Christ in a world of need.

FRIENDS TRANSFORMING THE LIVES OF OTHERS

One of our early supporters and dear friends in ministry is David Nelms. He serves as the director of the Timothy Initiative, a church planting movement that works to reach unreached people groups. He shared an update regarding one of the lives changed through his ministry's efforts that reminds us of the importance of reaching that one person in need of hope.

The Timothy Initiative student's name is Vincent, a 40-year-old husband with a wife and three children. He shares:

> I was an alcoholic for many years and felt awful about myself. I knew my habit was destructive, but I felt powerless to change. One day there was an open-air gospel meeting in the city where I work. I saw the crowd and was curious; I wanted to find out what was going on. It was at that meeting that I first heard about Jesus. After the meeting, the preacher shook my hand and gave me a gospel booklet. I took it home, but when I tried to read it, I needed someone to explain it to me. There was no one I could ask. I didn't know any believers.
>
> A few months later, I went back to my village. One day, on a school property, they were having an open-air gospel meeting. I saw the crowd. I saw a phone number for the pastor listed on a poster. I jotted down the number but decided against going to the meeting. A few days later I called the number. I later found out that the pastor was a Timothy Initiative district leader.

I invited the pastor to visit my home. I had a lot of questions that needed answers. My family was desperate to see me live without my drinking habit. The pastor came and shared his testimony with me. I shared about my drinking problem. The pastor prayed for me, and I was totally delivered. From that day on, I didn't have another drink. My family was amazed. They had lost hope that I would ever live without this addiction.

My deliverance gave me an opportunity to share Christ. Many people wanted to know how I overcame alcoholism. I called a meeting of friends and family to share Jesus with them. The pastor joined me and we shared the gospel with about 30 to 35 people. Many people were healed and delivered that day. We started meeting regularly in the community shed, which is the only suitable place to meet as the huts in our village are too small for a group our size.

God is working mightily among my people. Most of the people in this village are very poor and illiterate. Please pray for this village and for my people.

His life was changed through the efforts of a group of people committed to faith in action. Through the transformation of one life, many other people have come to know Jesus and grow in Him.

YOUR TURN

Faith alone is necessary for salvation. Action alone equals service. Faith and action combined equal a powerful impact. A book can serve as a great tool for information and inspiration, but it will only change the lives of others through your action. Let's talk together about five areas to address as you seek to implement compassion to people in need where you are.

First: ask, "What am I already doing?" You are probably doing more than you realize already. Consider how God is already working through your life. Is there a kid who is friends with your child at school whom you help out often? Do you serve with the prison ministry at your church? Are you the neighbor who is always helping other people with their yard work? Whatever it is, consider how God could use what you are already doing to impact others in a greater way.

Many of my skills are based in communications. As a result, when we first launched Relevant Hope, I wrote or edited the text for just about every piece of literature we sent out to local news networks, donors, or online readers. Jimmy has great networking skills and quickly connected Relevant Hope's work with other non-profits and churches in the area. We have another volunteer who uses her cooking skills to coordinate a weekly hot meal that we take to our homeless friends in outlying areas. The easiest place to begin is with the abilities you already have and the opportunities where you already serve. Build on these areas to consider how God would have you more deeply reach people where you live.

Second: look for existing needs. There are always more needs than there are people to meet them. Look for needs not already being met by others as your opportunity to serve. For example, with Relevant Hope, we have no central facility for people to gather, and we cannot easily meet this need. There is, however, a tremendous need for friendship among our area's poorest residents. We have chosen to go to those we serve, build relationships, and help on a personal level. When we run into needs we can't meet, we look for people already helping in those areas and work to make connections.

Third: experiment. You will likely need more than one try to figure out how God will best work through your life to reach others. Accept the freedom to experiment with a few options before choosing one long-term. In our efforts, we encourage potential volunteers to visit a camp with us before they decide whether to serve. They usually discover very quickly whether direct assistance with the homeless is something they can do effectively. If this area doesn't work, we suggest other options, ranging from organizing our storage facility, directing a fundraising event, connecting us with new churches and civic organizations, or even spreading the word on social media.

Fourth: build on initial success. Once you find your "sweet spot" in serving others, focus more time in this area. I'm much better at public speaking than I am at repairing cars. I've helped on a few small car repairs, but I try to find someone who actually knows what they're doing to come to the rescue. One of our volunteers who leads homeless worship services is Jeff. He is a contractor by profession and even wears a stocking cap that says *Jesus* on it during the winter. How is that for representing Christ?

On one occasion, a property manager in the area felt led to donate a rental house to Relevant Hope. The idea sounded great, but Jimmy and I had no idea what it would take to make it livable or how to proceed. Jimmy called Jeff for a visit. One quick look from Jeff gave us the answers we needed to move forward in providing another housing opportunity for our area's homeless. By building on his expertise in construction, he contributed to the work of Relevant Hope in powerful ways.

Fifth: follow God's leading. Not every opportunity can be neatly explained on paper. Sometimes God works through the principles outlined above, but sometimes there are surprises. For example, when I first moved from Indiana to Chattanooga several years ago, I had no family or friends in the area. My goal was to work at an organization that was making a difference and raise my family well. Taking a step of faith led to meeting Jimmy and the creation of Relevant Hope, a movement visited by ministers from as far away as Indiana who want to start something similar where they live. This experience has been one of those examples where God has been "able to do immeasurably more than all we ask or imagine" (Ephesians 3:20).

HOW FAR WILL YOU GO?

When it comes to helping those in need, the key question I've learned to ask myself is, "How far will you go?" Early into our efforts in serving people on the streets, Jimmy and I both faced personal financial problems. We could have easily stopped giving our time and money to help the poor in order to help alleviate some of our own needs, but we didn't. We decided we were fully committed to the cause. Nothing would stop us from giving everything we had or doing everything we could do to help people living outside.

In addition to our income, God often challenges us in other ways. Some of you may be challenged to start learning Spanish, equipping you to minister to Spanish-speaking immigrants entering our country. Others may be led to become more involved in your local government to support and assist officials as they face civic challenges (and, 1 Timothy 2:1–4 commands all of us to pray for our leaders). Maybe you need to learn guitar, start a food drive, hold a yard sale and give the money to the poor, or give a car or home to someone in need.

When the Apostle Paul wrote the Corinthian Christians about giving, he didn't focus on an amount. He focused on their willingness: "For if the willingness is there, the gift is acceptable according to what one has, not according to what one does not have" (2 Corinthians 8:12). God knows when your bank account is low and when you've worked a 60-hour week and can't help other causes. He understands your limitations better than you do. God desires a heart that is willing to help and committed to service.

Jesus gave all He had to show us His love. He not only died on the Cross; He gave more than 30 years of human life on earth to show us how to live. He showed us how to obey our parents, to work a job, to treat our neighbors well, and to participate in our community. He taught us how to serve others, teach others, and ultimately, how to suffer for others. We may not be called to die for others like Jesus did, but we can learn from the many other ways He devoted His life to show love to those around Him. Let us rise above the political and spiritual divides of our world and serve the Master whose kingdom is not of this world and whose reign will last forever.

CHAPTER 3

TAKING SCRIPTURE SERIOUSLY

YOU MEAN YOU REALLY BELIEVE THIS STUFF?

—————— JIMMY TURNER ——————

The homeless programs coordinator for the city of Chattanooga traveled with me one afternoon to visit homeless camps. She was new to the job and wanted to see what we do and how we interact. At the same time, she was hoping to connect with more of the homeless population and gather information that would help her with her job. As I dropped her off at City Hall when we finished, I asked her the same two questions I ask everyone when I take them to visit homeless camps for the first time: "Is it what you expected?" and, "What did you think about it?"

Since she had worked for years with the underprivileged, I wasn't surprised when she said that she expected to see exactly what she did from the people we visited. Something did shock her system a bit though, and it had nothing to do with seeing people living under bridges and out in the woods. She was most surprised by how I interacted with our outside neighbors.

"You spoke to them as if they were your equals and not people you were trying to help," she remarked. This one response allowed me an excellent opportunity to talk more in depth about why we do what we do in the homeless community.

MORE THAN FEELING GOOD

I've met a lot of people who want to do something to help in the community. They will volunteer at a local soup kitchen or Salvation Army during Thanksgiving and Christmas, they will prepare goody bags to give out to people in need, and they will tell you how wonderful you are for helping the less fortunate. What I've found most striking, however, is that they often do these things because they want to feel like they have done something good. In other words, whether they realize it or not, much of their motivation is to fulfill their own sense of self-worth or emotional satisfaction.

Over the course of winter 2014 to 2015, we eagerly worked to raise funds for a special kind of coat. This isn't just any coat; it is a coat that also doubles as a sleeping bag (you can see pictures at EmpowermentPlan.org). A young woman in Detroit named Veronika designed the coat and opened a nonprofit organization called the Empowerment Plan where she hires women from local homeless shelters to manufacture the coats. Her thought was that the coat wasn't enough; she also wanted to employ the very people who would need the coat.

As part of our effort to raise the funds for the coats, which are $100 each, we asked churches and other social groups that helped us in the past to commit to a certain percentage of our goal. One of the groups helped us raise $500 toward the purchase of five coats. This accomplishment was incredible by its own right, but the fact that the group who raised the money for us was the largest atheist social group in our area was even more surprising.

We were thrilled to have them help with our efforts, but something struck me when I was talking to the person who was responsible for collecting and transferring the funds. She commented that they were glad to "do something that made them feel good." There is nothing wrong with doing something that makes you feel good, but there has to be a more objective reason to sustain your motivation to action. Why? Because when the emotion wears off, so does the motivation.

As I spoke to the programs coordinator from the city, I explained to her that we do what we do because we have an objective reason that motivates us. Because our motivation is objective, we can put our emotions aside to accomplish the work. More importantly, the objective reason for our work also dictates the way in which we interact with the people we serve.

PEOPLE MADE IN GOD'S IMAGE

First, we serve the most vulnerable people in our community because all people are made in the image of God. When we read Genesis 1:26–27, God is the one who says "Let us make mankind in our image, in our likeness. . . . So God created mankind in his own image, in the image of God he created them; male and female he created them." There are plenty of theological books out there to explain *what* it means that we are image bearers of God, but I'm more concerned about *why* it matters that we are image bearers of God and how we apply that truth in our daily lives.

In Genesis 9:6, God said, "Whoever sheds human blood, by humans shall their blood be shed; for in the image of God has God made mankind." Simply put, your life is forfeit if you take another human life because of the intrinsic value of that person, who bears the image of God. The point is that human life is of tremendous value to God. This value includes every single life, regardless of background, skin color, or status.

Second, we are all equal in God's sight. We firmly believe each person is of invaluable worth to God and to us. Everyone has something to teach us if we are willing to learn. We understand those principles about people for two reasons. We observe that people are different from one another and bring unique perspectives. Further, we have the Bible as an objective authority in our lives. Paul wrote to the Philippians, "Do nothing out of selfish ambition or vain conceit. Rather, in humility value others above yourselves, not looking to your own interests but each of you to the interests of others" (Philippians 2:3–4).

Working with people who are homeless will open your eyes to a world of innovation you never knew existed. Early in 2014, I was making visits to some of the camps during an extreme cold bout. Temperatures were in single digits with wind chills below zero. One of the camps I visited is located under a bridge in downtown Chattanooga. The men living in the camp had acquired a Dutch oven. They had rigged together some tarps and blankets in such a way that they had a living room-type area outside of the tent next to one of the support walls for the bridge. They had positioned the oven in such a way to maximize the amount of heat they could build in their living room area. They had also arranged the blankets and tarps in such a way as to allow the smoke to rise up and out and still keep the heat in. When I walked into their camp, I was able to take off my coat and sit comfortably in their living room while it was nearly zero degrees outside. One of the guys in the camp had his shirt off because of how warm it was in there.

That kind of genius is nothing short of amazing to experience. As I looked at their set up, I could see the ingenuity and thought behind what they were doing. I was also humbled because I know that I did not know how to duplicate this effort. My life experience and education had not prepared me for what they faced. They were the experts, and I was willing to admit it and learn from them.

Their value as image bearers is enough to earn them my respect. But add their genius and expertise into the mix, and I'm left without excuse to treat them "above myself" as Paul wrote. I'm not out there helping people because I am trying to get something out of it. I'm out there because they are image bearers of God who deserve respect and dignity. I believe the Bible enough not just to give lip service to this ideal but to get out there and do what it says. If I follow Paul's words and look at others as above me, then I will also never have the opportunity to look down on anyone or treat them with any disdain. These are not homeless people we are helping; they are people who happen to be homeless.

I find it hard to listen to someone tell me that God has called them to help only a certain type of people. God doesn't call us to serve adjectives; He calls us to serve people. He may call us to serve people who are part of a particular demographic, people group, or set of circumstances, but we can't identify people merely by their adjectives. We must see them as people made in the image of a holy God, recognize the circumstances of their life, and serve them accordingly.

THIS IS SERIOUS

We do what we do because we believe the Bible. When I was finishing my explanation to the city programs coordinator about why we do what we do, I was disappointed when I should have been encouraged. She made the comment that out of all the years she had worked in social services, she has always noticed an attitude of superiority in service providers. That observation wasn't to say that they weren't well meaning and didn't honestly care about the people they were helping, but she said there was always a moment when watching someone that you could catch a glimpse of superiority for doing what they did. Then she looked straight into my eyes told me that she never once got that impression from me.

Her words shocked me. I struggle with pride and an entitlement complex as much as anyone else. Sometimes I have to work extra hard in this area, reciting Paul's words to myself as a reminder that I should approach others as though they are above my station in life, even if we classify them as the "least of these" in our community. I was also disappointed because I thought to myself that I am not the person anyone should look to as a standard of practice. I am just trying to be like Jesus. I can't even echo Paul's words, "Follow my example, as I follow the example of Christ" (1 Corinthians 11:1).

I had a professor in college who used to say that if we knew him the way he knew himself, then we would never want to be around him. That is how I feel when it comes to serving the kingdom. I know where I fall short on a daily basis, and if I ever forget or wonder where I'm falling short, I can just ask my wife or kids! The authenticity in our home is not a way for us to abuse grace. Rather, we want to know that we can always be who we are and know that our family loves us no matter what. If there is something in our life that needs correction, then we want that correction to happen in the safety of our home with the people we trust the most.

James 1:22 is such a clear-cut passage of Scripture: "Do not merely listen to the word, and so deceive yourselves. Do what it says." We are talking about a passage of Scripture that any Christian or even an unbeliever can understand, and yet we have deceived ourselves for years in the church to think that all of our services,

Bible studies, small groups, and Sunday School classes are what define us as mature and growing Christians. We've changed the goal as if the standard of maturity in our faith is based on what we know rather than what we do.

A local pastor was talking to me one day about the years of schooling, testing, and other hoops he went through for ordination in his denomination. While we were discussing this process, he recalled a day when a mutual friend said to him, "You know . . . you people sure do know a lot, but you don't do anything." He told me those words have never left him. He admitted that, to him and many others in his denomination, head knowledge had become a higher standard than obedience. His education had replaced his application.

James warned us that knowing a bunch of stuff can be deceptive. Paul echoed this statement when he wrote, "Knowledge puffs up" (1 Corinthians 8:1). Paul and James both followed up those statements with the same command using different words. James wrote, "Do what it says." Paul wrote, "Love builds up." Jesus offered this same teaching to His disciples: "If you love me, keep my commands" (John 14:15). Later, He shared, "Anyone who loves me will obey my teaching" (v. 23). He was clear that obedience was an expectation; it was not an option.

LIVING BEYOND EMOTIONS

Paul wrote that love builds up, and when we read 1 Corinthians 13, we discover love is about how we treat someone instead of how we feel about them. There is an objective basis of service instead of an emotional one. Love means I am going to serve you regardless of my emotions toward you.

A new client named Cathy called me one Friday afternoon to ask for a tent. This is not unusual. We are the only agency in Chattanooga that will provide tents to the homeless community as part of our normal outreach. This is one way we work to provide temporary shelter since Chattanooga lacks adequate shelter space for the number of people who've been designated as homeless.

I explained to her that we were waiting on a shipment of tents to come and that she needed to call back later. She was fine with that, and explained that the tent was for her and her boyfriend. Like many others, Cathy kept calling me back several times a day after she found a spot where she wanted me to bring her a tent. I had to make her wait temporarily since we did not have our shipment of tents, and her impatience grew with each call. As soon as the tents came, I sent Kevin, our director of operations, to the area where Cathy said she was staying to set up her camp along with those of others who were in need. Cathy was nowhere to be found for several days.

Later that week, Kevin and I stopped to visit some people at the Chattanooga Community Kitchen. We found Cathy and asked her if she was ready to set up camp. She was and went to find her boyfriend to let him know we were there and ready to help. John, her boyfriend, came back with her and told us that they had been staying in an abandoned house down the road. We loaded them up in our vehicles and took them to the house where they were staying to get their belongings. John told me that they didn't have much because they had only been around for about six or seven days.

When we pulled up to the pale green houses that were marked for demolition because they were condemned by the city, I was grateful to know that even though they were going from a house to a tent, they were going into a safer environment. I told them to load their belongings in the back of my vehicle since they didn't have much, but after the fourth trip with still more to go, I was starting to wonder how much "not much" really was.

Load after load kept coming until I had to ask Kevin if we could start putting some of it in his vehicle. Then John came out of the house carrying a bucket toward my vehicle. I knew as soon as I saw the bucket what it was, and I was not about to let it go in my vehicle. I asked him if it was his urine bucket, and he said, "Yes, but I wash it out every morning." I told him he wasn't sticking that in my vehicle no matter how often he cleaned it out!

We got everything else loaded and start to pull off when Cathy asked John if he remembered the tent. *What tent?* I thought. Without saying anything, I stopped the vehicle and waited for him to run back inside and come out carrying a tent. As soon as he was back in the car, I asked why they called me for a tent if they already had one. He claimed that they had just received it. I was beyond mad at this point, but we pulled away and drove down to where they were going to set up camp.

We got there and started unloading. The first thing that fell out of the back of my car was John's urine bucket! I was so angry that I just wanted to get their stuff out of my vehicle and leave. We finished unloading it, and Kevin drove his vehicle off road to get back to their campsite since his vehicle was all-wheel drive.

I rode with him back to the campsite and helped him unload the stuff from his vehicle when I saw John walking down the path carrying the first load of their belongings. He brought the tent in the first load, and I put my emotions aside to start putting together the tent he acquired. Prior to seeing him walk down the trail, I told Kevin everything that had happened, why I was so mad, and that I was going to leave them with their stuff to set up on their own. By God's grace, the Holy Spirit compelled me to stay and not give up.

We pulled the tent out of the pouch and started to unroll it. I immediately noticed something was wrong. I couldn't find the tent poles. Internally, I laughed because I knew this was why I was still there. We looked around for a minute and could not find the poles anywhere, so I asked Kevin to get the tent from his vehicle so they would have somewhere to sleep since their tent didn't have poles. Then, after the tent was set up, we put up a tarp for them to give their tent some extra protection and helped them get a few other things together in their camp.

When we finished, I pulled Kevin aside for a moment of confession. Here I was supposed to be the leader in the group, and I didn't want to live up to the very principles I was preaching to others. I wanted my emotions to dictate my motivation instead of Cathy and John's intrinsic value as image bearers of God. I told Kevin how I was feeling, and we talked through it for a minute until I reached a sense of peace with God that I had confessed my sin and He had forgiven me. I cleared things up with John as well and apologized for being angry with him.

"Do what it says; if you love me, keep my commands; love builds up; anyone who loves me will obey my teaching" (James 1:22; John 14:15; 1 Corinthians 8:1; John 14:23). These verses all came to mind, plus one more: "Whoever claims to love God yet hates a brother or sister is a liar. For whoever does not love their brother and sister, whom they have seen, cannot love God, whom they have not seen" (1 John 4:20). Just about anyone would have told me I was within my rights to walk away and let Cathy and John set up their own camp, but how can I claim to serve people on the objective basis of their intrinsic value as an image bearer of God if I walk away because of my emotions? How can I claim to love God if I'm not living out my love for the man and woman who are in front of me? It's not about emotion; it is about being obedient to Christ regardless of my emotions.

That's really the essence of our calling as believers. We are to put aside ourselves for the sake of Christ and His kingdom. If I walked away from that situation and had not helped them, it would be like telling God that my emotions and subjective reaction were more important than the value He gave Cathy and John.

By the way, Cathy and John are now living indoors and are engaged to be married. They are regularly attending church and working. That change in their lives is because we were able to continue serving them while they were homeless. I hate to think what might have happened if I let my emotions guide me that day instead of Jesus. We are called to take God's Word seriously, even when it is inconvenient or, maybe, *especially* when it is inconvenient. When we do, God changes our lives and the lives of others, often in unexpected ways.

TAG, YOU'RE CALLED

FOR MANY ISSUES, YOU ALREADY KNOW GOD'S WILL

DILLON BURROUGHS

I still remember the day Jimmy first shared his desire to reach the homeless of our community. He was about to graduate from a Christian college, and I was curious about what he planned to do when he finished. His goal? It wasn't a plush ministry job in suburbia; Jimmy wanted to serve the most vulnerable people in our community.

Part of why I remember this conversation so vividly was because I had just been praying about the same thing. I worked at a Christian media ministry in the area and had been involved in several missions trips to serve those in need, but God continued to challenge me to do more to serve the less fortunate in my own community. So when Jimmy shared his dream to change the lives of the homeless, I began to wonder if it was an answer to my prayers as well.

We met for coffee once, then twice, to discuss the church's role in helping the poor and how this role is often neglected. After about three times of meeting to talk, we came to one major conclusion— we didn't need more talk; we needed to start doing something.

The next time we met was an experiment of sorts. We prayed, drove to where he had heard homeless people lived, and started looking. Our biblical focus was simply the story Jesus told of the shepherd leaving the 99 sheep to find the one sheep that was lost. No matter what it took, we would find someone in need and seek to express the love of Christ.

Our first stops were unsuccessful. Jimmy twisted his ankle on a hill at our first stop, and the first two locations we visited had long been abandoned. We were about to give up and try another day, but neither of us wanted to stop. Jimmy knew of one other spot across town where a police officer had spotted a homeless encampment. We decided to make the drive and give one more attempt before ending our journey.

After parking near the underpass, we walked past stacks of tires and around trash calling out, "Good morning. Is anyone here?" To our surprise, one man sat in a recliner next to a massive beam that supported the bridge. He called himself Tree.

We didn't know it at the time, but Tree was our "lost sheep." As we mentioned in the introduction of this book, Tree became the first person we had the opportunity to lead to faith in Christ and to baptize. He now lives indoors, has a job, and volunteers with Relevant Hope to reach other homeless people in our area.

WHAT DOES GOD WANT ME TO DO?

One of the most common questions I hear from Christians, both young and old, is, "What does God want me to do with my life?" We want to serve God and help make a difference but lack direction regarding how to begin.

I personally struggled with this issue for years. When God was ready for me to take action, I figured He could give me a sign or send me a text message, but I've learned through both Scripture and experience that God's "burning bush" experiences are not everyday events. Even Moses and Abraham only had such encounters on a few occasions. Why should we expect something more?

If God doesn't usually speak to us in an audible voice or some major sign in the skies, how does He let us know what to do? The answer is found in the book that most Americans own, yet only a small percentage seriously read. The Bible offers clear direction on many areas of God's will. We don't have to ask God whether it is OK to cheat on a test or skip work or steal a car. God's Word is clear on these topics, and yet it is also clear in many other areas we tend to neglect. It took one of our generation's greatest natural disasters to truly awaken me to this lesson.

FROM HAITI TO HOME

On January 12, 2010, an earthquake devastated Haiti, killing 200,000 people and displacing and injuring countless others. I served with a disaster relief team in Haiti just days after the earthquake and witnessed tragedy and hopelessness at unprecedented levels.

My friend Andrew and I served at Mission of Hope, only three kilometers north of the mass graves covering more than 110,000 corpses transported from the nearby capital. Inside the safety of the mission, a different attitude existed. People still lived in tents, and medical emergencies continued to complicate the situation, but the people remained upbeat and positive about what was happening on their 76-acre compound.

We began by dropping off our luggage at the guesthouse and unloading our medical supplies and infant formula at both the clinic and orphanage. A few minutes into our orientation, Dr. Cheryl, the doctor from Canada serving the mission on a long-term basis and director of the clinic, received a call reporting that United States military helicopters had patients on the way. Mission of Hope's clinic, we had been told, was one of only a handful of medical facilities where General Hospital in downtown Port-au-Prince was sending their massive overflow of patients. Within less than 30 minutes from the time we had arrived, Andrew and I were carrying stretchers from military helicopters into the clinic for emergency treatment.

I cannot express in words how it feels to sprint up to a roaring chopper, reach out to pick up a stretcher, and realize the person I am picking up is missing a body part. Most of our eight patients flown in that day were amputees or had broken femur bones that had remained untreated for days. Our medical team instantly began the process of treating amputations for infection, casting broken bones, and providing other necessary services to save the lives of those entrusted to our location.

Of course, the patients flown in via helicopter were not the only patients. Others were brought in with the clinic's only ambulance or by truck, with a few people simply dropped off at the front gate. That afternoon, a young man who looked about 17 years old arrived with his left arm missing just below his shoulder. While this patient was in excellent physical condition otherwise, the earthquake had left its permanent mark on him. His wound was cleaned, pain medication was given, and we then moved him to the next building down, an elementary school now converted into what the clinic called "post-op" for care of patients after their initial treatment.

The next day included similar work. We served at the clinic where we carried the stretchers of more amputees and broken femur bone patients into the clinic's triage area. One helicopter turned into two and then three, with about eight total patients and their family members. The remainder of that Saturday was a blur. We helped move amputees from stretcher to bed, from bed to their operations, from their operations onto either the ambulance or a delivery truck to move into the "post-op" school building for recovery. At one point, I helped two other guys transport five different people into a delivery truck who were either on stretchers or in wheelchairs because our ambulance was busy taking a different patient to another hospital. The delivery truck was all that was available, and new patients needed their space.

On our last full day in Haiti, we rode with a local resident to see some of the damage in other parts of the nation. We first stopped at the mass grave area just south of Mission of Hope near Titanyen. The unmistakable smell of death rushed through my nostrils. I had seen dead bodies before, but I was not prepared for the decaying flesh at my feet from an earthquake that had happened over two weeks ago. It was January 31, 19 days since the earthquake that had started this tragedy. I walked speechless across the rubble that covered more than 100,000 people whose remains rested below the rocks where I walked. I could only think, "mourn with those who mourn" (Romans 12:15).

Our drive also included a stop outside of the capital building. No other place illustrated the widespread devastation better than the scene outside the presidential palace. Haiti's equivalent of America's White House had collapsed. We stepped out of our vehicle, and I experienced another smell—one I will not soon forget—the smells of the living—food, urine, human excrement—all mixed together among the voices of thousands of souls living in conditions I would not wish on my worst enemy.

At this site, we spotted naked people bathing in buckets of water. Children urinated on the sidewalk only steps away from where we stood. Most men and women simply walked around in a hopeless stare, not certain if they would live to see another day.

From there, we headed back to the mission, but not before driving through Cité Soleil, the poorest slum in the poorest country in the Western Hemisphere. Our driver passed quickly through this area because he had been carjacked there in the past.

In the days that followed my return to the States, I struggled with my return to "normal life." Didn't God want me to do something more? Something else? Anything? His answer was closer than I expected.

TEACHING AND LEARNING GOD'S WILL

After my trip to Haiti, I had many requests for interviews and speaking engagements to talk about my experiences. I felt completely inadequate as I had only helped for a short time, and so much work remained. Furthermore, I was leading my own family, working, and often struggling to keep my daily life together. How in the world was I supposed to help anyone else?

During this time, I stopped to spend some deep time in prayer and reflection with God. I admitted my inadequacy and feelings of being overwhelmed. In my moment of weakness, He remained faithful. It was through this period of struggle that God revealed three important principles I have since shared with many who likewise struggle to know and do God's will.

First, start where you are. This principle sounds obvious and perhaps too simple, but it is one that is often overlooked. We often want to give our lives for "big" causes, serve the unreached on the missions field, or start a megachurch or international ministry to change the world and reach every person on the planet for Christ. A closer look at the interruptions in Jesus' life shows the vital importance of serving when and where you are.

Luke 8 offers a great example. As Jesus walked with Jairus to the home of his sick daughter, a large crowd surrounded Him and "almost crushed him" (v. 42). The passage continues,

> *And a woman was there who had been subject to bleeding for twelve years, but no one could heal her. She came up behind him and touched the edge of his cloak, and immediately her bleeding stopped.*

— vv. 43–44

Jesus could have just kept walking. After all, He was on His way to heal a dying young girl. Instead, He stopped. He asked, "Who touched me?" (v. 45).

When the woman realized she had been noticed, she "came trembling and fell at his feet. In the presence of all the people, she told why she had touched him and how she had been instantly healed" (v. 47).

His response? Grace. He answered, "Daughter, your faith has healed you. Go in peace" (v. 48).

This wasn't the only time Jesus paused from His busy schedule to help someone in need. When Jesus was leaving Jericho, a blind man named Bartimaeus shouted for help. Mark 10:48 states, "Many rebuked him and told him to be quiet, but he shouted all the more, 'Son of David, have mercy on me!'"

Bartimaeus would not give up. He couldn't even see Jesus, but he knew He was near. He continued calling out above the noise of the crowd.

How did Jesus respond? Two words: "Call him" (v. 49).

Jesus then asked, "What do you want me to do for you?" (v. 51).

The blind man answered, "Rabbi, I want to see" (v. 51).

Jesus immediately healed Bartimaeus, and we are told he "followed Jesus along the road" (v. 52).

When Jesus was interrupted, He started where He was and helped those in need who were nearest to Him. There is always another mission "out there"—the next cause, the next city, or the next country that seems to be the most important mission we could pursue. Jesus illustrates that our greatest mission is often the person in front of us.

We know the Great Commandment calls us to love our neighbor as ourselves (Matthew 22:37–40). Yet many of us live in locations where we do not even know our neighbors. We have hundreds or even thousands of "friends" on social media but fail to address the hurts of those right next to us. Jesus calls us to start where we are. Sometimes, as with Jesus, this beginning continues with additional service in other locations. Other times, starting where we are can become an entirely new mission.

Second, do what you can. The same week Jesus would hang on the Cross, a woman came to Jesus during a meal "with an alabaster jar of very expensive perfume, made of pure nard. She broke the jar and poured the perfume on his head" (Mark 14:3). Her desire was to show love to someone who had impacted her life.

Not everyone understood. The text continues,

> *Some of those present were saying indignantly to one another, "Why this waste of perfume? It could have been sold for more than a year's wages and the money given to the poor." And they rebuked her harshly.*

> —vv. 4–5

How did Jesus respond?

Leave her alone. . . . Why are you bothering her? She has done a beautiful thing to me. The poor you will always have with you, and you can help them any time you want. But you will not always have me. She did what she could.

—VV. 6–8, AUTHOR'S EMPHASIS

God often brings those final words to mind in my efforts to serve the homeless: "She did what she could." There will always be those who question our motives, strategy, or efforts. We often place upon ourselves feelings of inadequacy and the need to do more, and yet, Jesus offers the proper perspective. He is more concerned about us doing what we can than how outsiders respond. Jesus cares more about our effort than our accomplishments. He knows our motives and our limitations. He doesn't call us to fix every problem or to please every person; He calls us to do what we can.

During one of our early worship services at a homeless encampment, an older man told me he could really use a Bible with larger print. They had Bibles, but the words were too small for him to read. I then showed him my own Bible I had taught from that morning and asked, "Would a Bible like this have large enough print for you?"

"Yes, that's exactly what I need," he replied.

At that moment, I sensed what God would have me to do. I put my Bible in his hands and said, "It's yours." He was shocked at first, not wanting to take a "minister's Bible." I insisted, departing from the camp that morning, leaving behind a man who had access to God's Word that he could immediately read and apply.

Yes, it was one of my favorite Bibles that I had used for several years, but I had others. He had an immediate need, and I did what

I could. At the time, there was no way to know whether he would throw it in the trash or read it from cover to cover.

The end result? A few months later, I attended this man's baptism at a local church after he was off the street. When we were sitting in church together that morning before his baptism, I looked down and there it was—my old Bible. He had been reading it regularly. God had used this one small effort to transform a life in a big way.

On another occasion, someone donated a giant, 12-person tent for some people on the edge of town who were staying in the woods. We took a few people from a local church and decided to bring breakfast and have a church service together. The only problem? There was no one to lead music.

I was hesitant to commit since I had just started playing guitar again after years of the instrument sitting in my closet. That morning, we hiked the winding, muddy trail to their tent and began to serve food. As the time neared to begin our worship service together, God convicted me about my fear of playing guitar.

To be honest, I was pretty scared. I had not prepared and didn't have music with me, but my guitar was in the back of my minivan in the parking lot of a nearby grocery store. I excused myself, jogged back to the parking lot, and returned with the guitar in my hand.

With a short prayer and a leap of faith, I gathered a small group of people into the tent and started playing. In God's grace, the songs I happened to know from memory were ones people from the visiting church knew. We worshiped God together in a unique and intimate setting that morning. Afterwards, the people staying in the tent were overwhelmed with emotion, saying, "I can't believe people care enough to do this."

Today, that tent no longer stands in the forest of our community. Those living in it have found new faith and have moved on to permanent housing, living with purpose and hope.

I wish I could say every attempt to do what I can ends up this great. Honestly, there are more failure stories than successes, but when I realize that God only expects me to start where I am and do what I can, I have no excuse but to try. God is in control of the results, and even one story of a life changed for His glory is worth it all.

Third, endure till the end. A one-week missions trip can change your life, but it does not teach you endurance. It was not until I began working with Relevant Hope that I learned this third valuable lesson at a deep level. After a few months of regularly searching for homeless encampments, climbing under bridges, and stopping to talk with every homeless person I could find, fatigue set in. Worse, I realized there would be no quick end to this pattern. This town was my home. I could not leave this "missions field" and return home for a break. It was a missions trip that never ended.

Part of this realization truly scared me. I knew my strength was limited, and I could not last at my current pace for long. During this time, God reminded me of the words of the Apostle Paul who wrote to the struggling members of the church of Galatia, "Let us not become weary in doing good, for at the proper time we will reap a harvest if we do not give up" (Galatians 6:9).

That verse became my new theme: "Do not grow weary in doing good." I needed to slow down sometimes, but I could not quit. Why not? The changes I desired for those in our homeless community were close at hand, but would not come if we gave up early.

These words were easier to say than to do. Our first winter, I remember waking up at 5:30 a.m. to pick up breakfast and drive out to some of our homeless camps. When I turned on my van, the temperature was three degrees, not counting the wind chill. I scraped the ice from my windshield, jumped back into my vehicle, and thought, *What in the world am I doing?*

I showed up as usual, offering help and hope to a handful of guys under a bridge. Our team also served at a nearby extended stay hotel that morning where we helped to house some individuals during the coldest nights of the year. One of those who stayed there was a woman with her three children. I thought to myself, "Where would this family be right now without this room?"

Another room housed two guys we often served at a nearby underpass. Instead of wondering if they were alive that morning, I knew they had just finished waking up from a warm night's sleep. We prayed together and spoke briefly, making sure they had what they needed to make it another day.

No revival broke out that morning, but God made it clear: "Do not grow weary in doing good." Despite the coldest winter in our city in the past 20 years, to our knowledge not a single homeless person died outside from exposure.

WHAT ABOUT YOU?

Like me, you may have a heart to help but don't know where to begin. I encourage you to *start small.* It was Mother Teresa who said, "Small actions done with great love change the world." If you know of one person who needs help to stay in his or her home, do it. If you have a friend who is struggling to make the payment on his or her rent or mortgage, help with the payment, or gather some friends who can each contribute. No project is too small or unimportant.

Second, work together. Any large problem worth taking on is worth taking on together. When we started Relevant Hope, we were committed to being a volunteer-driven, community-building movement. Our goal was not an office or warehouse. We are not out to compete as the city's top provider of services to the homeless. We're just here to help.

As a result, other organizations enjoy working with us and are unafraid to refer appropriate people our way. When the city of Chattanooga conducted its first ever Registry Week, part of Mayor Burke's initiative was to end chronic veteran homelessness. Registry Week is part of the 100,000 Homes Campaign that has seen an 80 percent success rate in other cities to eliminate chronic homelessness. Registry Week concluded with a great event at Miller Park, where area service providers came and met with many from the homeless community to initiate benefits and other services. Jimmy took the lead with the committee for targeted communities and worked with the city's Geographic Information System (GIS) team to develop a city map with many known camp locations to help volunteers find our outside neighbors. As a token of good will, the city turned over maps to Relevant Hope to maintain at our own discretion.

The result? Relevant Hope may be one of the only organizations in the nation that has mapped the entire homeless population of its community by location and individual people. This effort is not an attempt to track the homeless for safety concerns but is due to our heartfelt longing to know where people stay who are in need and help them move forward in their lives. In a sense, it is our high-tech version of the story of the lost sheep, where we make every effort to find that one last person on the street who needs hope.

Third, dream big. In our community, here are the facts about homelessness: there are more than 1,000 churches in the Greater Chattanooga area and a little more than 600 homeless people on any given night. It doesn't take a degree in statistics to calculate that if each church took care of one homeless person, homelessness would disappear in our town immediately.

I often challenge churches about this idea. I say, "What if every church in our town took responsibility to get one person off the street?" This challenge is dreaming big. What is the one question that could transform where you live?

Fourth, speak out. Find your area of passion and sound the alarm. Proverbs 31:8–9 instructs, "Speak up for those who cannot speak for themselves, for the rights of all who are destitute. Speak up and judge fairly; defend the rights of the poor and needy." When is the last time you spoke out for someone in need? I'm not talking about a general, "We need to help the poor" or, "Someone needs to share the gospel in the Middle East." I'm talking about a personal, passionate cry for specific people in need. When God gives you a passion for a particular cause, there is a reason for it, and that reason is not to keep it to yourself. You are called to be a representative for those in need. Do not fear. Speak out for the rights of the poor and needy.

Fifth, do something. Sometimes people like to complain about how we operate or tell us better ways to help the homeless. I always like to ask them what they are doing to help the homeless in the community. Usually, the answer is nothing. My response? "When you help, you can do it however you want. I prefer trying over talking."

James 2:16–17 teaches this principle:

> *If one of you says to them, "Go in peace; keep warm and well fed," but does nothing about their physical needs, what good is it? In the same way, faith by itself, if it is not accompanied by action, is dead.*

Talk is cheap. We all know people who speak about how much they are doing, but do so for personal gain or to draw attention to themselves. Jesus calls us to serve to meet the needs of others, not our own needs. Yes, it is a blessing to give rather than to receive, but the goal is action, not attention. We are called to help, not to hype.

One of my favorite passages in the Bible is 1 John 3:16–18. It reads,

> *This is how we know what love is: Jesus Christ laid down his life for us. And we ought to lay down our lives for our brothers and sisters. If anyone has material possessions and sees a brother or sister in need but has no pity on them, how can the love of God be in that person? Dear children, let us not love with words or speech but with actions and in truth.*

ALL IT TAKES IS A COUCH

During my last year of college, I had a conversation with a friend named Allan who had a problem—he had nowhere to live. He was a student but had to leave his dad's place and didn't have anywhere to stay. My roommate Chad and I quickly responded, "You can have our couch. Stay as long as you'd like."

He did. Allan stayed almost the entire semester.

During that time, we built a better friendship and encouraged one another. When he moved, I missed him and hoped his new place would work out. Three years later, I discovered he was graduating and moving to attend seminary. He ended up becoming a campus minister to students at the University of Notre Dame and is now married and raising a young family. His life has changed the lives of many others to live for God.

My roommate and I can't take credit for what happened in Allan's life. We do, however, get to enjoy how God worked through someone we helped. When we share our resources to help those struggling with housing issues, God often uses the experiences to transform us as well. The way I live is different because of Allan. The decisions I will make today have changed because of my times with the homeless of my community.

God's will isn't always written in the sky, but it is clearly written in His Word. When we act on what God has clearly revealed, we often find the direction we need for the other aspects of our lives. Who knows? Maybe discovering God's will for the next step in your own life is dependent on you engaging in the needs of your neighbor or your community in a deeper way. You'll discover this direction not by praying about it or talking about it but by starting where you are, taking a chance, and watching God at work in your life and in the lives of others.

CHAPTER 5

FOLLOWING THE GREAT COMMISSION *AND* THE GREAT COMMANDMENT

JESUS DIDN'T SAY, "CHOOSE ONE OF THE ABOVE"

JIMMY TURNER

My burden for working with people who live in the homeless community emerged from a short-term missions trip I took while I was in college. I was a nontraditional student and already in my late twenties by the time I enrolled. I had also dropped out of high school as soon as I was old enough to sign myself out and then went to my local community college where I obtained my GED. I married in September 2000, at 18 years old, and soon had two children. College was not an option for me at that time because I needed to provide for my family.

My father-in-law, David, recommended I work with him through the local electricians' union, which was a great job that paid well and had good benefits. I completed the journeyman training school for residential electricians and spent most of my electrical career setting services, wiring new houses, and troubleshooting the wiring in old houses. I made it about two years in that business before my wife and I moved from Tennessee to Alabama to live closer to my family.

FROM FAMILY TO MILITARY

The tragedy of 9/11 occurred two days after we moved. I was reminded of my time in Junior ROTC in high school and my lifelong desire to serve in the Marine Corps. Instead of enlisting, however, I started a job selling cars at a local new car dealer. I did OK as a car salesman, but my desire to move overseas and fight terrorists never left me. In April 2002, I signed up for the delayed entry program to join the Marine Corps. In May, I shipped off to Parris Island for boot camp.

I spent nearly four years in the Marine Corps before I was medically separated due to a developed condition that caused my heart to beat too fast. When I left the Marine Corps, I worked in a local jail as a corrections officer and then a corrections counselor. While there, I considered the idea of attending college, but I never knew what I would do with a degree or what I would pursue. After my job at the jail, I found out about a program available through Veterans Affairs where I could attend college for free. I was ready to sign up for anything.

FROM MILITARY TO MINISTRY

My educational pursuit began with a career in criminal justice. Only weeks into my first semester, however, I felt the call of God on my life to enter the ministry. I then transferred to Tennessee Temple University to pursue a degree.

During my time there, I thought God was going to let me finish school and then send me to serve as a pastor, but God had other plans. The year before I graduated, the school sponsored a spring break missions trip to Miami, Florida. I had not planned to go because I had a family at home, and I looked forward to the breaks from school to spend time with my wife and kids. One of the school's staff, however, personally came to me and asked if I would consider attending. I couldn't figure out why he wanted me to go, but I soon found myself on a bus to Miami.

On the way, we were told we would be helping the homeless, working at an orphanage, and assisting the Baptist Collegiate Ministry with outreach at Florida International University and the University of Miami. I was happy to do whatever I was told since I was getting a free trip to Miami and a new experience in ministry. But I have to admit, I wasn't expecting a napkin to change my life.

FROM MINISTRY TO ACTION

We drove into Miami Saturday night and had to be up Sunday morning to work at a place called Caring for Miami. It was a kitchen and resource center for those who are homeless and a place for those who wish to attend church services. Our team was divided into different duties while we were there. People were assigned to cooking detail, clothing exchange, preaching, security, evangelism, food service, dish washing, and other tasks. Given my background in the Marine Corps and corrections, I thought they would add me to the security detail. Instead, they assigned me to evangelism.

I'm not an overly shy guy. I can be the life of a party, speak in public without fear, and carry on a conversation. But after years in a church that used confrontational evangelism—a method that involves questioning individuals about their salvation without first establishing rapport or relationship—as its primary way of outreach, I was nervous to become involved in evangelism. My job was to walk around the kitchen, strike up conversations with people I didn't know, and help tell them about Christ.

As I looked around the dining area, my eyes locked onto a pack of napkins sitting by the door. I thought to myself, "Didn't Jesus often reach people by serving their physical needs first?" I grabbed a handful of napkins and started looking for people who were already eating and needed one.

As I walked around and found people needing napkins, I would offer them one. If they didn't say anything in response to my offer or just took the napkin without a "thank you," I would move on to the next person. As soon as someone would say anything in response to my request, however, I would use that as an opportunity for conversation. That experience changed my life and laid the foundation for serving the homeless in my community.

As I had opportunity to speak to each person who gave me an open door, my caricature of *homeless people* started to fall apart. Up to that point, I still viewed people who were homeless as bums, junkies, drunks, and the lost causes of society. I was raised in a poor family, and both of my brothers and I were able to work out of our situation, so why couldn't they? As I spoke with them, I realized that I'd never given these people the benefit of the doubt and that maybe there was more to their situation.

Person after person shared their story of broken families, lost jobs, depression, and other wounds that left me wondering why our society wasn't doing more to help. Then I experienced a moment of awakening in which I realized God was showing me how He wanted me to serve Him in ministry.

SAVED TO SERVE

God used napkins to teach me a lesson about evangelism. We are all called to make disciples, but we are also all called to love our neighbor. The Great Commandment and the Great Commission are expectations for every believer. Furthermore, when we consider the way Scripture discusses evangelism, it often uses images from farming and agricultural work, which means evangelism isn't simply an event where we invite people to come to faith in Christ. Evangelism is also a process by which we love our neighbor as ourselves and serve them in love by obeying Christ. Such actions open opportunities to present people with the good news of Jesus Christ.

I believe Paul said it best:

> *I planted the seed, Apollos watered it, but God has been making it grow. So neither the one who plants nor the one who waters is anything, but only God, who makes things grow. The one who plants and the one who waters have one purpose, and they will each be rewarded according to their own labor. For we are co-workers in God's service; you are God's field, God's building.*
>
> —1 CORINTHIANS 3:6–9

Ultimately, God alone gets credit for saving lives. Paul talks about building on a foundation and our buildings being tested by fire and rewarded for what survives (1 Corinthians 3:12–14), but what is the foundation and what are we building on that foundation? Paul tells us the foundation is Jesus Christ; what we are building on that foundation is our works.

The foundation of our faith is Jesus, and we build our works on that foundation. Those works are what we are doing as part of the Great Commandment, found in Matthew 22:37–40. Let's refresh ourselves just in case anyone forgot:

"Love the Lord your God with all your heart and with all your soul and with all your mind." This is the first and greatest commandment. And the second is like it: "Love your neighbor as yourself." All the Law and the Prophets hang on these two commandments.

"Love God; love people," is a simple summary to keep it in perspective. But didn't we read somewhere else that we have to do something first in order to say we love God? John told us, "Whoever does not love their brother and sister, whom they have seen, cannot love God, whom they have not seen" (1 John 4:20).

Bible studies and church services are wonderful, but our ability to love God is not based on how much of the Bible we have memorized; rather, it is reflected by how we have loved our neighbor. Again, 1 Corinthians 13 reminds us love is an intentional way we choose to treat others instead of how we feel about someone.

We can't neglect that Jesus also gave us the Great Commission as part of how we demonstrate our love for Him. What better way to show love for people and love for God than to serve the physical needs of others and then lead that person to a saving relationship with the God who sacrificed Himself to save them?

CHANGED AND TRANSFORMED

Scott was an alcoholic for more than 40 years. He would tell you that the past 40 years of his life was a fog. He has also been homeless for a large portion of that time. He has several medical problems that prevent him from working a regular job, but his contentment in his circumstances had also kept him from applying himself to obtain benefits that would improve his quality of life.

Scott was one of the first people we met when we started reaching the homeless in our community. He was also one of our biggest critics. When we first met him, he told the other people in his camp that we wouldn't keep coming. This didn't bother us that much because we know a lot of people show up talking about wanting to help and later quit because they don't have an objective basis for the work they are doing or simply don't endure.

As we continued to return each week, Scott needed a new reason to criticize us, so he made the comment to those in his camp that we were only coming to make ourselves feel like we were doing something. That was why we were always bringing stuff with us when we came. Up to that point, we were bringing something with us each time we would come to the camp. We brought breakfast, groceries, toiletry items, and other essentials. It wasn't because we wanted to make ourselves feel good. We were new at this outreach and didn't know what was most helpful, so we always brought something to give as part of our visit.

The funniest part about this entire situation is that while he was making these statements to the people in his camp, we weren't hearing any of it. The Holy Spirit is everywhere, and He guided our steps with everything we needed to do. I felt compelled one day to go visit Scott's camp just to see how they were doing and not take anything with me. When I pulled up to the woods outside their camp, Scott met me on the trail and asked what I had brought with me. I told him I had nothing, and he looked at me with a shocked expression. He threw his hands up in excitement and said, "Well, that's great! Come on in and just sit down and talk with us."

For the next several weeks, we would stop by their camp and only occasionally bring items we thought they needed. Other times we arrived with nothing but a smile and our company. Scott really started to open up during this time, but there was still something that kept him distant.

In spite of his coldness, the Holy Spirit was drawing Scott in. One of the other people we met made a profession of faith in Christ and we scheduled him to be baptized at our local riverfront. Scott and his whole camp attended with us because they wanted to support him in his baptism. When we got to the event, Scott pulled me aside and asked if he could be baptized, too.

I explained that baptism was something reserved for people who had made a profession of faith and then asked him if he believed Jesus is alive and would agree that Jesus Christ is Lord. He affirmed both. Then, I asked him if he believed he was in any way a different person because of Jesus being a part of his life, and he immediately said, "Yes, I know I'm different because of Jesus."

I told Scott that I would baptize him that day based on his profession of faith, but I also explained baptism was not going to save him or make him a better person; only Jesus could change him. He understood, and this alcoholic of more than 40 years walked down into the water with me and made a public profession of faith through baptism.

NEXT STEPS

In all of this, however, Scott still wasn't fully accepting of us. Once again, he made a comment to those in his camp and said that when it got cold we would stop showing up. In God's providential wisdom, He provided us with an example to prove Scott wrong with the worst winter our area had experienced in 20 years. I'll never forget the look on Scott's face when it was an unusually cold morning, around 14 degrees, and we walked into his camp at seven in the morning with breakfast and a guitar to have one of our on-site church services.

Scott really embraced his faith, and we could all see a big change in him as the months went by, but he was still drinking. As we were leaving his camp after a visit one morning, he turned to me and said he knew he needed to quit drinking but couldn't do it on his own. I asked him if he would go to a rehab facility if I could arrange it for him, and he said he would. I looked him straight in the eyes and said, "Scott, I need you to understand what I'm saying to you. I can't guarantee any advance notice of an available bed. I may show up one day and tell you it's time to go, and I will need you to drop everything right then and go with me." He told me he understood, and I had a mission.

FREED FROM ADDICTION

I learned that we have a state-run rehab facility in Chattanooga and did some research to find out what it took to get someone who is indigent into treatment. I showed up early one morning at Scott's camp and told him we needed to go. He immediately dropped what he was doing and was ready to leave. It was reassuring for me to see that he was willing to live up to his word.

We drove down to the referring agency and met with a case manager for evaluation. After he had completed evaluation, the case manager came out to speak with us together. She explained that he was approved for treatment, but we would have to wait for a charity bed to become available, and that could take weeks before he could get in. We accepted the process and left encouraged, knowing that he had an opportunity to get the help he needed to get sober.

The facility called and gave us a date of November 6 that he could check in for detox and admission to the rehab program. Scott and I celebrated the news, and he reassured me that he was going through with it no matter what. He told me his drinking was so bad at this point that he would open a beer at night before he laid down for bed just so he wouldn't have to struggle to open it in the morning before he was fully awake. There was not a waking minute of his day when he wasn't drinking beer or thinking about it.

November 6, 2013, arrived, and I was at his camp early that morning to pick him up. When I arrived at his camp, he was waiting at the edge of the woods with his bags packed and ready to go. He was so excited to know that his life was about to change.

It was probably 7:30 in the morning when I arrived to get him, but in the short amount of time he had been awake, he was already shaking from detox just from going the previous night without drinking. Help was coming at a time when he needed it most, and I was honored to help him through this process.

I took him into the facility and helped him check in, and then he was behind the locked doors. He wrote me a letter while he was in rehab that I still have locked away in my safe. When the day came for him to get out, I was filled with anticipation when I pulled up to the center to take him back to his camp. I met with his case manager, and we spoke at length about the spiritual and social support he would need. I committed to do whatever needed to be done to support him and help him stay sober.

As part of his personal recovery from being an alcoholic, he wanted to have a more traditional church home where he could be a member, so he returned to a church down the street from his camp where he attended once. The pastor of the church said he didn't even recognize him when he came back to the church. Everything about him was different, and the pastor was anxious to find out what had changed.

Scott told the pastor his story from meeting us the previous summer all the way to his rehab and then his desire to be part of a local church. The pastor was thrilled to have him attend and started including Scott in his mentoring with some of the other men of the church. After several months and many hard fought battles against temptation, it was evident that the changes Scott encountered were there to stay.

Not only was Scott attending church regularly, he was reading the Bible on his own and reading popular Christian books. He would still meet with us when we would have a service with the rest of his camp, and he always had questions to ask from his time in Scripture that week. We would spend hours talking about the Bible and ministry and Jesus. To this day, those moments with Scott in his camp are some of my favorite times in all the work we've done in the community.

FROM REJECTING CHRIST TO SHARING CHRIST

Scott soon picked up his guitar again for the first time in decades and started playing. He learned some of the songs they would sing at church and started to participate in the praise team on Sundays, but something was still bothering Scott. When I found out what it was, any doubts I had about whether his faith was authentic or just a crutch to get support completely withered away.

Scott and I met once or twice a week at a coffee shop to talk about life and Jesus. One day while we were sitting in the coffee shop, he looked at me with a serious face and said he felt like something was missing in his faith. He said, "All the church services and Bible studies are great. I love learning about the Bible and Jesus, but I feel like God wants me doing more than attend church services." He continued, "I believe I should be doing something to reach other people. This message of hope changed my life in ways you don't even know, and I don't think it's right for me not to share that with other people."

It was at that moment I truly understood that evangelism isn't an event we can mark down at a moment in time. Evangelism is a process that begins with the foundation of Christ and continues through the multiplication of disciples who join the kingdom. Scott knew he had a message with power behind it, and he wanted to share that message with others.

We worked with him for a while to start holding a small group in his camp, but he struggled with getting others to cooperate with him. Then he started searching for people to talk to about his faith but found little success. Exasperated, he came to me one day and said that he didn't understand why God would put such a desire to serve in his heart but not give him the opportunity to serve. I encouraged him to be patient and trust that the Lord had an opportunity waiting for him.

Dillon leads a couple of our homeless church services each week. One of them takes place on Friday mornings at the Chattanooga Community Kitchen. We prayed about it and felt like God was giving Scott an opportunity to speak at one of those services. On Friday morning, October 31, 2014, Scott preached his first message based on the testimony of what God had done in his life to an audience of about 50 homeless men and women.

Not long after his first message, Scott returned with Dillon to lead the music during another service at the Kitchen. Scott found an outlet where he could serve according to the skills God had given him, and he was a Holy Spirit-filled leader when he got up there, too.

BEYOND WHAT WE CAN ASK OR IMAGINE

As part of the 1-5-1 Harvest Field Plants Program, the Tennessee Baptist Convention (TBC) divided the state of Tennessee into seven "Harvest Fields." Each field is assigned a team that is responsible for training and equipping local TBC churches to reach the lost in their area through church planting and seeking people out of the context of their local church such as the homeless, poor, and others. As a "Harvest Field missionary," I recently planted a new church in Chattanooga called Engage Church. We met at my home for the first few months while we started a core group that would help build momentum. We then found a place we could start renting on a weekly basis for an affordable rate that was ready for us to use for services. The problem was that none of us were musically inclined enough to lead worship, though we all agreed we would be biblical by making a joyful *noise*.

I started looking around for a worship leader and no one could commit. As I was praying one day about this concern, God brought Scott to mind. I called him and asked if he was willing to lead worship for us in our inaugural service at our new location. After a long silence, he responded, "Are you sure you called the right person?" After assuring him that I meant to call him and to ask for his help, he agreed. He was excited to have this opportunity to serve, yet he was also terrified. In the end, he did an amazing job leading us into a fresh experience of God's love and grace that Sunday.

FULL CIRCLE DISCIPLESHIP

The Great Commission instructs us to make disciples, baptize them, and teach them obedience to Christ's commands. Christ told us the greatest commandment is to love God and love our neighbor, and John tells us that we don't love God if we don't love our neighbor.

The Great Commission and the Great Commandment are insep-arable. We obeyed the Great Commandment by building a relation-ship with Scott, but doing good deeds wasn't enough. Through the Great Commandment, we were able to share the gospel with him in a way he would understand, and God opened his heart to receive it. Then we were able to incorporate the Great Commission into our work by building him into a disciple, baptizing him, and then teach-ing him what Christ calls all Christians to do as we grow in faith.

If we went into his camp empty handed the first time we had met Scott and pointed out the sinfulness of his drunkenness, we would most likely have experienced nothing but rejection. We certainly would not have been invited back. There is an appropriate time and place to speak about the judgment of God and the seriousness of sin. Jesus, however, described discipleship as a process rather than an event. We began by showing Scott God's love, sought to meet his needs, and allowed God to work in his heart at the appropriate time to bring Scott to faith in Christ.

DEMONSTRATING GOD'S WORD

Do we believe the whole counsel of Scripture enough to do what it says? If we say we do, then we should demonstrate it. Remember the words of James, "What good is it, my brothers and sisters, if someone claims to have faith but has no deeds?" (James 2:14). This is a great example of what I see so often in churches from people who claim to be believers. They will acknowledge that someone is in need and offer to pray for them but then do nothing within their own ability to be an answer to their own prayer.

In the Book of Ruth, we see a great example of demonstrating God's Word. Boaz told Ruth, "May you be richly rewarded by the LORD, the God of Israel, under whose wings you have come to take refuge" (2:12). Later, Boaz was willing to take responsibility for Ruth by marrying her and providing her through his own ability with the rewards and refuge she sought.

How is that for the Great Commandment? Boaz wasn't just willing to pray a blessing over Ruth in love; he was also willing to fulfill it by using the resources God had already given him.

What would it look like in our communities if every prayer request in our churches was then followed by actions to answer these prayers? We can't neglect the Great Commandment for the Great Commission; neither can we ignore the Great Commission for the sake of the Great Commandment. They are links connected in the same chain we call evangelism.

CHAPTER 6

CTRL + ALT + DEL CHURCH

A FRESH LOOK AT CHURCH IN ACTION

——— DILLON BURROUGHS ———

Following the closing prayer, a woman sitting toward the front of the service said, "I needed that!" We had just completed our concluding message on 1 Thessalonians, encouraging people to live for God, giving thanks in all circumstances. We learned together, prayed together, and sang together. Afterwards, I had the opportunity to talk with several individuals regarding various struggles, praying with some and encouraging others. It was a practice I have participated in with many churches over the years.

Except this was no ordinary church.

Our church consisted of dozens of homeless people in a downtown day center at 8 a.m. on a Friday morning. Unlike most American congregations, we enjoyed a multicultural worship experience that reflected the ethnic diversity of our community. Instead of an auditorium, we had metal folding chairs. Instead of a stage, I used a simple music stand. No one wore a suit and tie or high heels. There was no record of attendance on the wall or banners with Bible verses. We had no bulletin, and it was not Sunday.

But it was church . . . and lives were being changed.

One man had just started a new job and said he might not be back next week. Another lady asked me to pray with her and her friend because her friend had recently discovered she had cancer. A gray-bearded gentleman sat in the back reading a Bible we had recently given him. Still others hung around for hugs, handshakes, or simply to talk.

It was church, but it was certainly not the image that comes to mind when most of us think of going to church.

Years of leading worship services in homeless encampments, tents, and day centers has led me to ask many deep questions about what church is and how it is intended to operate. What defines a church? Is it the steeple or the stained glass? Is it a certain time and day of the week when people meet to worship God? Our culture offers one set of answers to these questions. The Bible offers another.

When we look closely at the first church and other early churches in the New Testament, several themes emerge. Some of the concepts are familiar—preaching, prayer, communion, community, and evangelism—while others are not—meeting in homes, gathering at odd times, and sharing meals and life in a holistic manner where every person participates.

The churches of today tend to focus on the organizational aspects of life—such as the order of worship or the programs for children, youth, and adults. The churches of the Bible dealt with organizational issues, yet these topics served as only a small part of their focus. The New Testament church emphasized what God did *through* them, while some modern churches may tend to focus on what can be done *for* them.

In short, we have made ourselves the focus rather than Christ. Scripture, however, is clear that Christ is the head of the church.

Church leaders are shepherds who serve under His leadership, while all members of the church are family, brothers and sisters, who live life together to encourage one another and to reach those beyond the church with the hope of Christ.

TAKING CHURCH TO THE STREETS

Several years ago, my wife and I talked with a homeless woman named Rebecca. We had a decent conversation including some talk about spirituality. She was already connected with a local social worker and had a church home. We ended up encouraging her the best we could, but we felt highly inadequate to provide help beyond the moment. What could be done to help?

To be honest, Rebecca would not have felt comfortable in most churches. But what if we took church to her? It was not until my work with Relevant Hope that an answer began to emerge that could address the many Rebeccas of our community. It did not take long to discover that few of the homeless in our community attended traditional churches or would feel comfortable attending one. In fact, it was rare to find anyone among the homeless who attended church on Sunday. There were simply too many barriers in most cases. There was no car, no appropriate clothing, and no connection between the daily experiences of a person on the street and what most Christians experience on a Sunday morning.

From our earliest days, Jimmy and I sought to "take church" to everyone who was willing to spend time with us. We first began by showing up with breakfast and a Bible. We would eat together, share briefly from Scripture, and end with a prayer. Afterwards, we would always take time to talk together and really listen to the needs of those we served. We worked to meet needs and remove barriers that kept people from housing and hope-filled living. When we did, people were glad to have us show up. We weren't trying to only be pastors but served as friends who wanted to help improve the lives of our fellow neighbors.

During our first year, we launched more than a dozen outdoor churches, all under bridges or at homeless encampments. Our unconventional approach led to many interesting and sometimes humorous experiences.

For example, some of our congregations included smokers, dogs, and cats, and some of our sermons were regularly interrupted by passing trains. On another occasion, I arrived to begin our weekly gathering to find police searching for a criminal on the loose. Many services also took place in below-freezing temperatures or rainstorms. We've shared communion around campfires, baptized new believers in local lakes, and probably hold the world record for the number of church services held while trespassing on the property of others.

THE CHURCH WITH NO NAME

After nearly a year of trekking to every corner of our community to share God's love with those on the street, God opened a new opportunity. We were invited to hold a weekly worship gathering at the Community Kitchen day center. This location offers free meals to the poor and was located near where many of the homeless we were already serving. I said yes and showed up for the first time on the Friday after Easter in 2014.

My expectation was that a few interested people would join me around a table for a small Bible study. Instead, I walked in with my Bible and guitar and was presented as "the pastor" for the morning. I was given a microphone, a lecture stand, and the attention of the entire audience. To be honest, I was a bit intimidated. Breathing a short prayer, I led people in worship and encouraged people with God's Word. No major miracles took place that day, but a church was born.

Even today, nearly two years after beginning this weekly outreach, new people at the Kitchen ask me "what church I'm with." I just tell them I'm with Relevant Hope, and we're here to help encourage people who might not otherwise attend church. We are literally the church with no name.

But this anonymity doesn't mean we are not a church. We may not meet on Sundays, but we do worship the Lord. It just happens to be Fridays at 8 a.m. We don't have an offering, but people are regularly sharing their resources to help those in the greatest need. We don't have a steeple, stage, or membership class, but lives are being changed—one life at a time and one day at a time.

Last week, one of my "members" came up to me at the end of the service to share with me about witnessing to one of his homeless friends. This friend was a homeless veteran who lived in a tent, had overcome addictions, and continued to receive counseling for post-traumatic stress disorder (PTSD) and other issues. Yet he was telling me about his burden to share Christ with other people on the street! This man is a friend I look forward to seeing in heaven, rejoicing together over the many lives he is impacting today.

WAS JESUS HOMELESS?

There is a popular T-shirt I like that says, "Jesus was homeless." If you type a simple Internet search with this phrase, you'll find a wide variety of responses to this controversial statement. Was Jesus homeless? If so, how should this realization impact how we address this issue?

Let's take a look at the biblical evidence. First, Jesus was born in a manger, which means He was technically homeless on the day He was born. Shortly afterwards, His family fled as refugees to Egypt. As a child, His parents moved back to their hometown of Nazareth, where He grew up and likely worked as a carpenter until around the age of 30.

During His three and a half years of public ministry, Jesus travelled frequently. In fact, in Matthew 8:20 Jesus stated, "Foxes have dens and birds have nests, but the Son of Man has no place to lay his head" (also in Luke 9:58). This verse clearly notes that Jesus had no permanent address during this time. He operated as a traveling rabbi, either camping along the way or staying in the homes of others. On the night He was arrested, Jesus was staying outside in a garden. According to today's definition of *homeless*, Jesus would definitely fit.

Of course, this description does not mean Jesus was constantly in need during His teaching ministry. His followers would have supplied many of His needs for food or shelter. The Gospels record Jesus eating and teaching in the homes of others on many occasions, so it is likely He stayed overnight in some of these homes as well.

What stands out, however, is that much of Jesus' ministry consisted of living and serving among the lowest-income people of His society. He was born in obscurity and raised in a small town.

When Jesus died, He had no inheritance to divide. The clothing He wore on the night He was betrayed may have been some of His only earthly possessions. His focus was on a home beyond this world. In John 14:2–3 He promised,

> *My Father's house has many rooms; if that were not*
> *so, would I have told you that I am going there to pre-*
> *pare a place for you? And if I go and prepare a place*

for you, I will come back and take you to be with me
that you also may be where I am.

Jesus clearly focused on a home in heaven beyond this life.

This attitude regarding housing and earthly possessions offers much insight for our own lives. I remember once moving to a new town and attending a church for the first time. My wife and I visited a class with other married couples. The majority of the conversations before and after the class were about mortgage rates and housing prices. While these are important issues, I doubt Jesus would focus so much time on these topics if He walked into our churches today.

Instead, Jesus frequently spoke of a kingdom not of this world. He mentioned the kingdom more than 100 times in the Gospels. Following 40 days of fasting, Jesus returned to His hometown synagogue in Nazareth and shared these words from the prophet Isaiah:

> *The Spirit of the Lord is on me, because he has anointed*
> *me to proclaim good news to the poor. He has sent me*
> *to proclaim freedom for the prisoners and recovery of*
> *sight for the blind, to set the oppressed free, to pro-*
> *claim the year of the Lord's favor.*
>
> —LUKE 4:18–19

His goal? To share good news with the poor, the imprisoned, the blind, and the oppressed. Shouldn't this be our goal as well?

THE LEAST OF THESE

On another occasion, Jesus spoke about a group of people He called "the least of these." These were not less important people but those considered outcasts by society. He shared,

*For I was hungry and you gave me something to eat,
I was thirsty and you gave me something to drink,
I was a stranger and you invited me in, I needed
clothes and you clothed me, I was sick and you
looked after me, I was in prison and you came to
visit me.*

—MATTHEW 25:35–36

Notice the categories of people Jesus chose to highlight. They included the hungry and thirsty, immigrants, those in need of clothing, the sick, and the imprisoned. How many times have you seen headlines speaking against people in these categories today? You can probably think of several examples from the past 24 hours. These are the individuals of whom Jesus said, "Truly I tell you, whatever you did for one of the least of these brothers and sisters of mine, you did for me" (v. 40).

This compassionate service is what some people have called being Jesus to Jesus. Jesus says that when we serve the most vulnerable and forgotten people in our society, we serve Him. Scripture also teaches we are to be the hands and feet of Jesus, the body of Christ, to those in need (1 Corinthians 12).

I find this teaching far more motivating than the church growth seminars that are often promoted to churches. When our focus is on the most vulnerable in our society, we often find the greatest openness to God. Even better, as Jimmy will share in chapter 8, serving those in need attracts others who want to serve in these areas. Unbelievers who look at Christianity with skepticism can also find a new reason to look at God again when they see His people changing the lives of those in need.

GET DIRTY

In my work with people in the homeless community, few know about my other work. Though I have been given the opportunity to work with well-known authors and leaders and have written many books, my goal is not to market a message. Instead, I throw on my boots and get dirty as needed to reach those we serve.

When your goal is not fame or notoriety, you can simply show up, offer compassion to people, and let God do His work. Paul described this kind of lifestyle in Romans 12:9–16:

> *Love must be sincere. Hate what is evil; cling to what is good. Be devoted to one another in love. Honor one another above yourselves. Never be lacking in zeal, but keep your spiritual fervor, serving the Lord. Be joyful in hope, patient in affliction, faithful in prayer. Share with the Lord's people who are in need. Practice hospitality. Bless those who persecute you; bless and do not curse. Rejoice with those who rejoice; mourn with those who mourn. Live in harmony with one another. Do not be proud, but be willing to associate with people of low position. Do not be conceited.*

These commands drive our efforts. Like Jesus, we seek to serve rather than to be served (Mark 10:45). As the old church saying goes, we realize we may be "the only Bible some people will ever read." We want people to get the right story, respond to God's message of hope, and be changed.

One early morning, I visited a homeless encampment during a heavy rain that flooded the trail to the people I had come to see. By the time I finished, my boots were drenched, and mud covered my pants up to nearly my knees. Since I had to go to my office afterward, I quickly changed clothes in my van before showing up at work. That afternoon, I picked up my daughter after her piano lesson. She looked in the back of my van and asked, "What happened?" From an outsider's view, it looked like I had just completed a mud run and thrown my clothing in the back of my vehicle.

There was no course in seminary for this kind of ministry. No textbook taught me to take breakfast to people who are hung over in order to share the gospel or to climb under bridges to feed the poor. Only the love of God can cause a person to walk consistently and persistently with those in need in order to help them grow closer to God.

We find ourselves in ongoing contact with those whom society has rejected. Our goal as people created in God's image who are deeply loved by Him is to restore a sense of dignity. If it takes crawling through mud to show someone God loves them, then we must be willing to put on our boots and do whatever it takes.

JESUS DIED FOR THEM, TOO

Let's face it: some people are easier to love than others. It doesn't take long while working among those in need to find both those who are hurting and those who have hurt others. We've met murderers, child abusers, rapists, drug dealers, prostitutes, and others who have committed the most violent crimes imaginable. To be honest, it is sometimes extremely difficult to continue serving someone who admits they abused their girlfriend or shot someone in the past. We share two things with them: we are both sinners and Christ can change us both.

It is easy to say, "Jesus loves you." It is much more difficult to show someone the love of Jesus. When I struggle with serving others, I'm often reminded of Jesus on the Cross. In the midst of dying, one of the other criminals hanging on the cross next to Him resorted to mocking Jesus. The criminal on the third cross asked Jesus to "remember me when you come into your kingdom" (Luke 23:42). Jesus gave His life for the sins of the world—for both men—the one who would reject Him and the one who would accept Him.

We are not called to be successful; we are called to be faithful. This truth is difficult to accept in our success-oriented society. We long for recognition and fame or notoriety, but Jesus calls us to deny ourselves, take up our crosses, and follow Him. He compels us to leave the 99 to purse the one lost sheep (15:1–7). He calls us to accept every lost son who returns home like a loving father (vv. 11–31). These challenges are what shape us: "Do not conform to the pattern of this world, but be transformed by the renewing of your mind" (Romans 12:2).

BE THE CHURCH

My friend Charles Powell once shared a powerful story of a challenge he gave at a pastors' conference. He said, "Do you really want to reach new people for Christ? I will give you a method that I know for certain will help double the size of the average congregation in the next two years. Are you ready for it?"

The ministers sat up and prepared to take notes but were surprised by his next words: "Go to your church building, lock the doors, and take your church services to wherever the greatest needs are in the community. Focus on the homeless and the poor. Go to those who would never come to your church. In two years, you'll likely reach at least 200 new people who would never come into the doors of your church."

Charles's words describe what we attempt with Relevant Hope. We are not working simply to grow the church but to be the church. Many have sounded the call to "be the change you wish to see in the world," an idea popularized by Gandhi. We, however, can only change so much on our own. To truly make a dent in society's problems, we need a team. We must be the church we wish to see in our community.

How do we be the church where we live? Let me encourage you with some of the biblical principles we practice that help in our service to others.

First, begin with "two or more." Jesus taught in Matthew 18:20, "For where two or three gather in my name, there am I with them." Yes, God is at work in you personally, but it is when we join together with other believers in service that we transition from being the change to being the church. In our case, Jimmy and I became the "two or more" in the founding of Relevant Hope. Before we ministered to a single person, we prayed together, built a friendship, and talked about how we could impact the lives of others.

Though we both had a long-standing interest in serving the homeless of our community, neither of us had been successful in previous attempts on our own. It was not until God brought us together that we were able to gain the necessary momentum to launch, grow, and persevere through the many difficulties of a new outreach.

Even when there are only two people, there are still different roles to play. I have often joked that I see myself as Barnabas and Jimmy as Paul. He is the outspoken leader who charges ahead into new areas. I'm generally the guy who serves as the encourager and works to bring together ideas and people to maximize the impact of our efforts. Together we are able to reach more people in more places from different backgrounds than we could alone. Plus, we are able to keep each other going when the going gets tough. We've each had our times when we've wanted to quit or make poor choices. With another friend on board, we instead have a teammate to encourage us and help us see the bigger picture of God at work.

Second, start a group. In our case, we began with a single group of homeless people under a bridge in downtown Chattanooga. We made many mistakes during this time, and we learned a lot. While we initially wanted to speed up our efforts to reach more people, God used this first group of friends to help us truly understand the deep needs and concerns of those who experience chronic homelessness. We addressed addictions, broken family relationships, trauma, PTSD, and many other issues among this first group that opened our eyes to the genuine hurts and hopes of those on the street. If it had not been for those earliest friends in our small group, we would still be making the same mistakes among others we serve.

Most importantly, we learned to treat homeless people as people. They are not most importantly addicts, drunks, junkies, or even homeless; they are people. When you treat people well, they tend to respond well. These people are our friends and family. We don't just show up for an hour a week. We call or text throughout the week, stop by just to hang out sometimes, pray for one another, and share our own concerns about life. Together, we have built a true biblical community that transcends socioeconomic boundaries and focuses on loving God and loving one another.

Taking on any major problem often overwhelms us into doing nothing. If we focus on the crowd, we fail before we begin. Instead, focus on changing one life. You may not be able to end hunger in your town, but you can make one sandwich and give it to someone who needs it. You cannot solve the loneliness of every elderly person in your community, but you can spend an hour with someone in a nursing home or hospice. You will not heal every sick child, but you can volunteer at a children's hospital. You can't adopt every orphan, but maybe you can adopt one.

One matters. God gave His one and *only* Son. Jesus promised that whoever believes in Him—every individual person—will not perish but have eternal life (John 3:16). If you change one person and I change one person and every other Christian in every community works to help one person, many of our world's larger problems would resolve.

Third, reach others. This reaching includes both multiple groups and sometimes new areas of outreach. In our case, we began connecting with additional homeless encampments through our existing friends on the street. While homeless locations frequently change, we were soon connected with nearly the entire outdoor community.

Even better, some of the first people we served began serving with us to reach others. This stage began to reflect the biblical model of discipleship. Second Timothy 2:2 shares, "And the things you have heard me say in the presence of many witnesses entrust to reliable people who will also be qualified to teach others." Those disciples we first reached were helping us reach others who reached still others. The best ministry is multiplication, not addition.

Over time, some efforts yield better results than others. One camp we served initially no longer exists because everyone is housed or has moved out of town. In another camp, more people live there now than when we began. Our weekly service at the Community Kitchen has become a full-blown outdoor church. Some of our other camps only meet once in a while or not at all.

When we reach out to others, two things happen. We see God working on a larger scale, and we lose control of outcomes. These

CTRL + ALT + DEL CHURCH

transitions can be both exciting and frightening. I still remember when we first had volunteers leading new locations, and I did not even personally know the volunteers, much less the people they were helping. It didn't seem right that I was not there and was not involved, but the reality is that any one person is limited in the ability to serve others at a personal level. It is only with a team that outreach can extend beyond our limitations to become an entire movement in the community and beyond.

I find comfort in seeing this reality in the early church as well. The first church rapidly grew from 120 people to more than 3,000 (Acts 2:41). By Acts 4, there were more than 5,000 men who had become Christians (v. 4). Acts records no other numbers after this point, reflecting that the church's early growth was beyond counting. Churches were growing in number and size, with congregations soon sprawling across the Roman Empire.

By the later years of the Apostle Paul's ministry, he focused more on writing letters and developing leaders. He could no longer visit every church, start more congregations, visit more cities, or control every decision. Instead, he poured time into key people and into resources that helped the entire Christian movement.

Fourth, tell what God does. After Paul and Barnabas's first missions trip, they returned to their home church of Antioch. Acts 14:27 states, "On arriving there, they gathered the church together and reported all that God had done through them and how he had opened a door of faith to the Gentiles." Their goal was to share the stories of God at work.

A large part of our current efforts with Relevant Hope have begun to shift from doing to sharing. When God does something great in our lives, we naturally want to tell someone about it. In our case, God is doing something great in our community and, increasingly, across our state. We definitely want to share this good news with others and encourage Christians with how God is changing lives.

When God works through you, are you sharing the results with others? I'm not talking about the statistics or finances, though these details can be an important part of the story. I'm talking about communicating the good news of God changing lives for His glory. The verse preceding Acts 14:27 records, "From Attalia they sailed back to Antioch, where they had been committed to the grace of God for the work they had now completed" (v. 26). I find it interesting that this verse uses the phrase "the grace of God." Their work was a grace of God. It was not something they deserved or accomplished in their own strength. It was a result of God's favor through their efforts that lives were transformed in powerful ways.

The same is true in your efforts and in ours. When God shows up and the unexplainable happens, don't attempt to explain it as something you did. Tell the story of how God has worked through you to change lives by His grace.

Some time ago, a woman we helped sent us an encouraging note that said, "When I was homeless you helped my husband and me. Every Thursday you would bring us a hot meal to our camp. You people are all angels. I am so thankful for everything you did for us. We always liked to see all of your smiling faces. You were all so nice to us." If this family was the only one we ever helped, all of the effort would be worth it.

---- CHAPTER 7 ----

CONTROVERSIES 'R US

WHEN TAKING A STAND MEANS TAKING A HIT

———— DILLON BURROUGHS ————

When we arrived at Jackson's homeless encampment one morning, he was clearly angry. I walked over to ask him to join us for breakfast at the nearby campfire. Some new volunteers showed up that morning to visit, and I selfishly hoped for the morning to turn out well to give them a positive impression.

It didn't go well.

In addition to being angry, Jackson had not been taking his regular medication. A relationship conflict the previous day kept him awake throughout the night. He was furious, hurting, and exhausted.

I suggested to the new guests that they join the rest of the group and told them that we would join them soon. Jackson and I stood alone in the forest outside of downtown as he vented his frustrations while I listened. My goal was to let him get the anger out of his system until he could cool down and join the others. Since I could see he was carrying a knife, I had no plans to feed his anger and simply hoped to outlast his tirade. After several minutes, he paused to catch his breath.

I tried to offer some encouraging words during his break. They didn't work.

Instead, he responded with even stronger anger, threatening to take down me and everyone else nearby. Here I was, with no defense, no backup, and no plan. All I could do was pray.

So I did.

Jackson's outburst continued a bit longer with additional threats to beat me up. Though I felt confident I could shield myself from his attack, I was uncertain whether he would reach for his knife or how far I would need to take this encounter. He raised his fist, and I said the first thing that came to mind: "Is this really going to help?"

Jackson froze, pulled down his fist, and wept. He was a broken man who wanted help but did not know how to find it. Once I sensed it was safe, I walked up and reached my arms around him in a hug. We stood there for several moments as he allowed his emotions to run free that morning.

What began as a battle ended with hope.

UNCERTAINTIES ARE CERTAIN

When we began serving people who live outside, we knew there would be some controversial moments, but what we did not know was how often and how difficult these uncertainties would be. Jimmy has experienced three instances where people attempted to assault him because of their mental illness or intoxication and he had to defend himself. On another night, he visited a camp alone, which we don't normally do, that had about 18 people. All were convicted criminals, and the camp previously had situations where cops were called to respond to rape, assault, or attempted murder. When Jimmy approached, they started yelling, "Who are you?" When Jimmy identified himself, they answered he was pretty brave to show up there. Even cops did not walk into their camp without backup.

(It is important to point out that we have a policy that no weapons are allowed among staff and volunteers when going into camps. We intentionally leave ourselves vulnerable. Carrying weapons would make it much harder to gain the trust of people because they would know that we clearly don't trust them.)

On another morning, I showed up at a camp before sunrise where I said I would bring some breakfast and share a brief Bible study. We were sitting in the dark when I recognized a new guy in the camp. He told me he had just gotten out of prison and had shown up there last night. I think he was trying to scare me off by the way he said it. In most churches or even other contexts, sitting in a dark underpass with felons for a meal sounds a bit creepy. For me, I just welcomed him with some food and a handshake.

When cops search your congregations, or when your church services include an occasional fight erupting, you know you are no longer doing church as usual. As I read the accounts of early Christians, I find their efforts to share God's love included many risks that we rarely even consider. The Apostle Paul recounted his numerous dangerous encounters:

> I have worked much harder, been in prison more frequently, been flogged more severely, and been exposed to death again and again. Five times I received from the Jews the forty lashes minus one. Three times I was beaten with rods, once I was pelted with stones, three times I was shipwrecked, I spent a night and a day in the open sea, I have been constantly on the move. I have been in danger from rivers, in danger from

bandits, in danger from my fellow Jews, in danger from Gentiles; in danger in the city, in danger in the country, in danger at sea; and in danger from false believers. I have labored and toiled and have often gone without sleep; I have known hunger and thirst and have often gone without food; I have been cold and naked. Besides everything else, I face daily the pressure of my concern for all the churches.

—2 CORINTHIANS 11:23-28

Does God expect us to endure this kind of suffering to be a good Christian? Not necessarily, but God's Word does make a promise that many of us overlook. Second Timothy 3:12 plainly states, "Everyone who wants to live a godly life in Christ Jesus will be persecuted." I like to tell people that if you're not being persecuted in some way, you're not doing it right.

God does give times of peace in our Christian lives, but it is not all of the time. We can't claim to take on the most difficult issues in our community to share the love of Christ without running into some complications. The same struggles the missionaries who visit our churches face in their efforts in other nations should also show up in some ways in the ministries we conduct closer to home. The Bible shares many ways Christians can face persecution and suffering:

- Shame. (Hebrews 11:26; 13:13)
- False accusations. (Psalm 35:11; 27:12; Matthew 5:11; Acts 6:13; 16:19–23; 26:2, 7)
- Ensnarement. (Daniel 6:4–5; Luke 11:54; Matthew 10:16–18)
- Conspiracy. (2 Samuel 15:12; Genesis 37:18; 2 Corinthians 11:32; Acts 9:23)

- Mockery. (Psalm 42:3, Job 12:4; Matthew 27:29, 31, 41; Acts 2:13; 17:18, 32; Hebrews 11:36)
- Betrayal. (Matthew 24:10; Luke 21:16; Psalm 41:9)
- Being despised. (1 Corinthians 1:28; 4:10c)
- Hatred by family. (Matthew 10:21, 34–36; Micah 7:6; Luke 21:16)
- Hatred by men. (Luke 21:17; Matthew 10:22; Job 19:19)
- Being feared by own people. (Acts 9:26)
- Subjection to special trials. (1 Corinthians 4:9–14; 2 Corinthians 11:23–28)
- Imprisonment. (Luke 21:12; Acts 4:3; 5:18; 12:4; 16:24; 2 Corinthians 6:5; 11:23; Hebrews 11:36)
- Beating. (Acts 5:40; 16:23; 2 Corinthians 6:5; 11:24; Matthew 10:17)
- Threats. (Acts 4:18, 21; 5:40)
- Stoning. (Acts 7:58–59; 14:19; 2 Corinthians 11:25; Hebrews 11:37)
- Afflictions. (2 Timothy 3:11; Psalm 34:19)
- Exhaustion, extreme fatigue. (2 Corinthians 11:27)
- Hunger and thirst. (2 Corinthians 11:27; 1 Corinthians 4:11)
- Suffering physical need. (1 Corinthians 4:11; 2 Corinthians 6:4; Philippians 4:12; Hebrews 11:37)
- Martyrdom. (Luke 21:16; Acts 7:59; 12:2; John 16:2)

Have you faced *any* of these persecutions in your own life? You don't need to use these areas as a checklist, yet it is clear that those who seek to seriously live out their faith in Christ will face trouble. There will be some kind of conflict for people who wish to live for Jesus.

One of my friends in ministry serves women who dance in the adult entertainment industry. She works with a team to make sure these women are treated well, shown care and compassion, and are given help to escape if and when they are ready. Do you think a prayer request for this ministry might raise a few eyebrows at church on Sunday morning? It would be far easier to do something else, but she and her team clearly feel led to serve those women no one else in their city is reaching with the love of Jesus.

In my work in the area of apologetics, I've also run into some controversial situations. I've talked with Wiccan priests, shared Christ with radical Muslims, been called a heretic by a Jehovah's Witness, served near voodoo priests, witnessed to gangs in the inner city, and am still breathing and walking. As I tell those people we serve with Relevant Hope, if your heart is still beating, God is not done with you yet. You have been created for a purpose, and it's not to waste your life. We are called to live for God through times of peace and times of controversy.

UNHAPPY ENDINGS

During the first few months of our work, we met Darrell, a gentleman in his sixties who stayed with his son and daughter-in-law under a bridge outside of our town. He had been sick when we first found him. We offered to take him to the hospital, but he refused. Instead, we brought a tent, blankets, and food to help them until they could go somewhere else. We regularly stopped by to see if Darrell's condition had improved or if they were willing to go the hospital. Instead, we soon found out Darrell had died.

We had no idea what to do. All we could offer was to help connect his son and daughter-in-law with his family members from another part of the state to take care of funeral arrangements. We did, and later found out his son and daughter-in-law had moved into housing.

Darrell's death really rattled me. Here was a man we had helped, offered to help more, and regularly prayed for many times, but there was no happy ending. There would be no success story to share. His time was over.

Even in Darrell's death, God began to work in me in a deep way. Serving the poor on my city's street was not a game; this ministry was serious. Life was hanging in the balance. Eternal life was also hanging in the balance. The clock is ticking, and we are either wasting time or investing it to make a difference. Sometimes, when I don't want to wake up early to visit a homeless camp, or I feel sick or weary, the image of one man under a bridge who might die today without knowing God loves him motivates me.

TREAT PEOPLE LIKE FAMILY—BECAUSE THEY ARE

I've long developed a belief as a follower of Jesus in treating people like family—because they are. In one sense, every person is a brother or sister. God created all of us in His image. In addition, those who are Christians become our spiritual brothers and sisters. We are children of God who belong to the heavenly Father. I've found that applying this attitude toward those in need completely changes how I think about and treat them.

For example, if Darrell was my dad or my brother, what would I have done differently to help him? If the 65-year-old woman we found camping alone in the woods was my mom, how far would I go to help? If the guy I found passed out under a bridge was my brother, how would I respond? These are not just people; this is personal.

I still remember the words of one lady we met early in our work with Relevant Hope. The thing she remembered most? It was when we shared communion during our outdoor church services. Jimmy had decided to make fresh grape juice at home rather than to buy a cheap version of juice at a grocery store. She said, "Who does that?" It wasn't a matter of convenience; it was an act of love.

One Christmas, Jimmy, Kevin, and some of our other volunteers planned to take gifts and food to many of those we serve in the homeless community. To be more creative, Jimmy wore a Santa suit and other volunteers dressed as elves. Of all things, someone called the police because they looked suspicious! Of course they were. Who else would dress up in costumes to deliver gifts at homeless encampments on Christmas Day? The police officers had a good laugh when they realized what was taking place, but this visual example also showed how far the love of a few people can go to impact the community. The local news even ended up featuring our outreach.

On another cold morning last winter, a woman we met was staying in a shelter after fleeing a domestic abuse situation in another state. She had just been hired for a new job, but she was in trouble because her car battery was dead. There was no money to replace it, and she desperately needed the job to get back into housing. We found her a battery, a volunteer offered to purchase it, and I stood in the cold with her and two other guys who installed it The two guys who helped were also staying at the winter emergency shelter and lacked housing. This case is an example of everyone helping each other to get one person on the road to recovery.

When the project was complete, the woman was completely overwhelmed with emotion. "I cannot believe this is happening!" Our God leads us to act in ways that show an overwhelming amount of love to point people to the grace of our Lord.

These acts of kindness are not random nor are they easy; they happen, however, quite regularly among our volunteers and those we serve. If we need shoes for a kid or a tarp for a camp, we can put out an email or message on Facebook, and the item requested shows up. If one of our outdoor friends needs a ride to an interview, a driver volunteers. When food is needed, someone on the team steps up and shows up with it hot and ready. Each act is both a blessing to God and a testimony that God is still working through everyday people in extraordinary ways.

BE THE NEWS YOU WISH TO SEE IN THE WORLD

We have talked about being the change you wish to see in the world and even being the church you wish to see. But have you ever considered this concept in terms of news? Our daily headlines are generally filled with death, doom, political scandal, and other negatives that can discourage those who follow the news closely. Every once in a while, major news outlets will highlight a positive trend or story in our culture. Have you ever thought about making the news instead of just watching it?

As Americans, we probably watch more television or online videos by the age of ten than we need for an entire lifetime. Just working during the commercials we watch could add thousands of hours of productivity to many of our lives. I've made a commitment to watch very little television and instead invest my time in my family and helping others. Why? When Jesus returns, I seriously doubt He'll ask me if I've caught up on the last season of *Game of Thrones*. Personally, all I will want to do is bow before His throne. I don't want to look back on life and wish I had gotten off the couch more. My goal is to hear God say, "Well done, good and faithful servant" (Matthew 25:21).

Where do we begin if we want to shift from apathy to action? *It begins on our knees.* Jesus prayed and fasted for 40 days before He launched His major years of ministry. Why should we expect to simply walk out the door and make a difference without consulting with the God we long to serve? After returning from my trip to Haiti after the earthquake, I prayed for several years before Relevant Hope became a reality. While I worked in other areas along the way, both my prayers and those of Jimmy and others prepared the way for the work we do today.

Second, connect with those you desire to serve. You can't help the homeless from a distance. You must spend time with people who live outside. If you want to help those in prison, go to a prison. If you want to help those in hospice, go to a hospice center. If you want to serve children, go to a program that helps children. As you pray, you must connect.

Upon my return to the States from Haiti, it was difficult to readjust. The two dollars I spent on a cup of coffee was the amount the average Haitian made in an entire day of work. The amount I spent out on a meal with my family was enough to support a child for a month. Every purchase was suddenly physically painful. Every time I turned off my lamp at night, all I could think of was how blessed I was and how little I was doing to change the situation.

As I sought to change, I found an article in my local newspaper that mentioned the many people in my own city who were homeless. I may not be called to move to another country, but my community had needs as well, and they were needs I could do something about.

One of my experiments included contacting the local Habitat for Humanity. Amazingly, they had filled all of their housing construction volunteer teams for the rest of the year. So I looked to downtown Chattanooga at the Community Kitchen. Like many Americans, my schedule was already full, but when I asked where they needed help, they needed volunteers to serve breakfast. So I did. That commitment meant waking up at 5:30 a.m. to get there on time, but every week for an entire summer, I scooped oatmeal and poured coffee for many of our community's homeless citizens.

While I enjoyed this service, I longed to do more than offer food; I wanted to give hope. What I realize now was that my initial effort was to serve a need rather than to connect with people. I was kind to those I helped, but my only contact with them was for a few seconds in a food line. Jesus fed people on occasions and calls us to do so as well, but the far greater need of most people is for one true friend.

Third, be consistent. One-day outreaches are not enough. Without consistent involvement in the life of another person, we limit the impact we can have. Most of the people we serve need anywhere from several weeks to several months before enough trust is built to have a full friendship where they will open up about their personal life. When they do, you soon discover why they hurt so deeply. I've had people tell me about watching friends or family members die in front of them or about the abuse they experienced as a child. Others have never known their father. Some have experienced divorce or addiction that sent them on a downward spiral and led to life on the streets. Every story is different, but you don't get to hear the whole story unless you remain consistent.

Fourth, become family. When I meet with those we have served for some time on the streets, we greet one another with a hug. They are family. In fact, for many of those we serve, we are the closest family they have. If they had anyone close in their biological family, they would probably be living with them instead of outside.

I can't tell you *how* to become family with those in need. All I can say is that prayer, connection, and consistency can lead to a friendship that becomes like the community God intended for His people. You become, as Proverbs 18:24 says, "a friend who sticks closer than a brother."

WHEN PERSECUTION COMES

Despite our best efforts to live at peace with those around us, there will come times of trial or persecution. How can we respond during these times?

The first way to respond effectively to persecution is to expect it. The Christian life was never intended to be easy. One of the greatest lies about Christianity is that if we faithfully follow God, He will bless us with health, wealth, and prosperity. A close look at the Bible destroys this myth. Jesus was perfect, yet He faced ridicule, arrest, beatings, and death. The Apostle Paul was the greatest missionary of the early church, yet he faced numerous sufferings. History records that he was beheaded for his faith in Rome. Tradition states the Apostle Peter was crucified upside down for his faithful Christian life. These and many other examples clearly illustrate faithfulness does not equal peace and prosperity in this life.

Early on in our work with Relevant Hope, we had to decide whether we were willing to face criticism and even persecution to live for Christ and help those in need. Sometimes the concerns dealt with legal issues. For example, homeless encampments are typically on someone else's property. Entering these locations is technically trespassing, which could result in arrest or fines.

As we have mentioned, there are also safety issues. I don't usually give out my personal phone number or home address for a reason. Most of my visits are in the morning hours when people are less likely to be high or drunk. Our visits are generally in teams of at least two, especially when first entering new locations. We take precautions to avoid attacks, but there is no perfect system if we intend to go to those in need.

There are also character attacks that can occur when serving those in need. Remember when Jesus was called a friend of sinners and tax collectors in the New Testament? Those words were not intended as a compliment. He was also accused of casting out evil spirits by Satan's power. In Matthew 11:19 and Luke 7:34, Jesus was called a glutton and a drunkard. Jesus was accused of all kinds of crazy faults, though He was sinless and did nothing wrong.

Why should we expect anything less when we seek to help the most vulnerable people in our society? We've been accused of enabling drunks, addicts, and abusers. Some have thought we were just doing it to feel good about ourselves. Others claim there are plenty of other people helping the homeless, and we're just wasting our time.

I love what 1 Corinthians 5:9–10 says about this concern:

> *I wrote to you in my letter not to associate with sexually immoral people—not at all meaning the people of this world who are immoral, or the greedy and swindlers, or idolaters. In that case you would have to leave this world.*

Unless we plan to sign up for a trip to Mars, we will continue living on a planet filled with sinners, ourselves included. Rather than avoid contact with every sinner, we are called both to live pure lives *and* to take the good news to those in greatest need. Being a friend of sinners was not intended as a compliment for Jesus, but maybe it should be when people make such accusations of us when we help the poor.

The second way to respond effectively to persecution is to embrace it. What do I mean by this statement? Romans 12:21 urges, "Do not be overcome by evil, but overcome evil with good." When we expect persecution, we can embrace it when it does happen. We encounter evil, but we do not have to be overcome by it.

During one of our Friday morning worship services, a young lady came in shouting that she loved Jesus. As I played guitar, she jumped around like a cheerleader, trying to get everyone to stand up and participate in the songs. She caused quite a disturbance that morning, and I soon discovered why. When she came near where I stood, you could smell alcohol on her breath from several feet away. I was disappointed at her display but not surprised.

After playing music, I specifically looked her in the eyes when I asked everyone to sit down and join me as we read Scripture together. I silently prayed, read from the Bible, and proceeded to share as I usually did. As she rested, her energy seemed to fade. By the end of our time together, many prayed with me regarding living God's will for their lives that day, seeking His good above all else. God may allow a disturbance, but we don't have to be disturbed by it. We can overcome evil with good when we continue to show both truth and love without reservation and without conditions to those we serve.

LET'S GET PERSONAL

Let me be very personal with you for a moment. I did not attend seminary to crawl through the woods to share the gospel with the poor. My thoughts were on growing a church that would stand out in a community and serve as a model for others who lead churches. It has taken much time for me to realize how misguided my early desires were for Christian service. Yes, God called me to ministry, but He did not call me to become a celebrity or run a large organization. He called me to show His love to those in need.

I'm learning more than ever the power of Jesus's words, "It is not the healthy who need a doctor, but the sick. I have not come to call the righteous, but sinners" (Mark 2:17). Church may be primarily for believers, but the gospel is for all people. If Jesus came to seek and to save the lost, if He came for sinners, if He came to touch the untouchables and love the unlovable, how are we to live? Are we not to strive for a similar attitude and lifestyle? Shouldn't our maturity in Christ lead to doing harder things, going to more difficult places, and taking on more challenging efforts?

Why is it that new Christians are often those with the most passion to serve while those who have been believers for years lack similar desire? Is it perhaps because they have not really matured in faith? James said those who hear God's words and do not act upon them are deceived (James 1:22). You are fooling yourself if you have read the Bible from cover to cover and you do not care more for the lost and hurting and broken than you did before you read it.

I know. From the age of 17 until a few years ago, I continued the goal of reading through the Bible at least one time per year. At a certain point, I realized reading was not having the same impact as in the past and felt led to start writing out the Bible by hand. I called it the Holy Writ Project. Within three years I had written out every word of my Bible. Did writing the words change me? Yes, but not in the way I expected. I thought I would remember Scripture better and memorize more verses. Instead, God fundamentally changed my heart for Him and for others.

The closer I grow with God, the more I want to stop spending money on cable television or vacations or clothes and use it all to help those without hope. As I truly learn about the love of our Lord, I want to spend more time with those in the worst situations. My heart longs to show kindness to young people and the elderly, to offer encouragement to the addicted, the disabled, and the immigrant. I don't care as much about titles, but I care about the stories of God changing lives one by one.

A close look at the Gospels reveals that the word poor is mentioned 25 times. We read examples like, "Blessed are the poor in spirit, for theirs is the kingdom of heaven" (Matthew 5:3). We find Jesus challenging religious leaders, "Be generous to the poor, and everything will be clean for you" (Luke 11:41). We read Jesus teaching His disciples,

> *Sell your possessions and give to the poor. Provide purses for yourselves that will not wear out, a treasure in heaven that will never fail, where no thief comes near and no moth destroys. For where your treasure is, there your heart will be also.*
>
> —12:33–34

What else are we to take away from Jesus' teachings in these and many other passages than that one of the best uses of our time is to invest in those who have the least? If our time and income and use of abilities reflect our heart for God, then a closer look at these areas can reveal whether or not our heart reflects His.

When our hearts overflow with love for God and for others, we care deeply when others hurt. We mourn when others mourn. We read the headline of those who have died in an earthquake or war or hurricane and grieve for their loved ones. Most of all, we stop passively watching the injustices in our world and actively engage in doing something about the wrongs around us. What does God require of us? Micah 6:8 says, "He has shown you, O mortal, what is good. And what does the LORD require of you? To act justly and to love mercy and to walk humbly with your God."

TOGETHER WE CAN

APPLYING SCRIPTURE IS A TEAM SPORT

JIMMY TURNER

After presenting our work with Relevant Hope to a local church, the pastor stopped me and said, "You know, Jimmy, you talked a lot about how to focus on building relationships with people instead of programs, but I notice that you are also relying a lot on the programs of other agencies." He got it! Relevant Hope is built on providing on-site service through relationships, but we intentionally work together with other organizations to help far more people than we could ever reach on our own.

"Together We Can" is the battle cry we take with us into the community. To meet the many needs among the homeless in just my own community requires case managers, mental health experts, and many others. We have made it our goal to *serve with our community to serve our community.* The results have been amazing. Chattanooga includes hundreds of nonprofit organizations, ministries, churches, and social service providers. We have found it much more beneficial for us as an organization and for those we help to use people already equipped in other areas than to work solo and do it ourselves.

I've invested tens of thousands of dollars in my education. I have a bachelor's degree in biblical studies, a master's degree in ministry, and I am currently working on a PhD in leadership. I hope that people would come to me because of my education and expertise rather than trying to figure out the Bible or ministry on their own. In the same regard, I don't pretend to be an auto mechanic. Mechanics go to school and receive regular training to keep up with the advancements in automobile technology. If I try working on my car, chances are I would make it worse than it already was and leave the mechanic with more work to complete. I know because I've tried! My wife, Shay, reminds me, "I told you to take it to the mechanic in the first place." Honestly, even though it can be expensive, I would rather have a well-trained mechanic work on my vehicle. He is the expert and knows when he finishes the job that it is done. I know that if he makes it worse, then he has to fix it, and I don't have to pay for it. I enjoy the peace of mind that knowledge brings.

It is the same way with my taxes. Between house payments and interest, charitable giving, and all of the other aspects involved with my taxes, I would much rather pay an accountant than find myself audited by the IRS. My accountant knows how the system works, how to complete the process more efficiently, and how to reach the goal of completing my taxes accurately and on time.

We often recognize and utilize this approach with experts in various areas of business, yet we often fail to work together with others to help with the human needs that exist before us.

Where I live we have an organization called the Chattanooga Community Kitchen. They serve three meals a day, provide a day center where people can hang out during the day, offer case management services to those in need, and provide many other great services. Yet on Saturday mornings, there is a guy who sets up right across the street from the Community Kitchen to serve hotdogs. He offers a free meal to homeless people outside the doors of a homeless shelter that is already serving free meals. Wouldn't it make more sense to donate his hot dogs and his time together with the Community Kitchen instead of setting up his own cart? I'm sure he means well, but when you set up outside of a nonprofit organization and offer the same services they are offering inside, it gives the impression that you want people to notice what you are doing more than you want to help.

Our goal isn't to be noticed but to be effective. That is why we don't try to invent new ways of doing what is already happening in our community. We are the only organization that regularly provides tents and tarps to the homeless community. It is well known in our area that if a homeless person needs a tent, they can call us and get help. The only requirements are that they must have their own place to set up the tent, it must be at least three months since the last time we've given them a tent, and they have to let us come out to set up the tent with them. Why? First, we don't want to be responsible for telling someone to set up a camp in a location that is not ours to oversee. We also use a black marker and write the person's name on the tent so no one will sell or trade it for something else.

Often a homeless friend will tell us someone stole his or her tent, and then we find it at another camp. We'll ask the new owners how they got it, and they will claim to have purchased the tent from the person to whom we gave the tent initially. Then we go back to that person and tell them we found their *stolen* tent and have already notified the police of the theft so they can arrest and charge the responsible individual. Usually at this point the story changes, and the truth comes out. The silliness of the whole situation is astounding. The other person could have just asked us for a tent, and we would have given it to him or her. Instead, he or she bought the tent from someone who received the tent free from us.

We set up the tents for a couple of reasons. First, it guarantees that we will know the owner's camp location by going to their camp and setting it up. This way we can follow up with them regularly to develop a relationship. Second, we know that the tent was set up and not given away or sold. Third, we take the spare parts from the tent with us when we leave so they can't take it back to the store and get our money back for the tent. Ever heard the expression that rules are made because someone actually did the action described? Well, we didn't need these guidelines for giving away tents when we first started, but we do now.

ONE BODY, MANY PARTS

My friend Barry Kidwell is the director of Mustard Tree Ministries, an outreach that provides services to the homeless through meals, church services, and other arrangements. When I met Barry, he was serving soup at a park downtown to anyone who wanted it. There were probably 150 people at the park that day. Many were homeless, some were from a nearby public housing facility, and others came by during their lunch break from work. It was quite an experience the first time I visited.

Dillon and I sought Barry because he was the one name that kept coming up as a person who served the homeless community in Chattanooga. Brother Barry, as he is affectionately known, was rumored to leap tall buildings in a single bound through his work. He has served in the inner city for more than a decade, providing meals and church services throughout the week at different locations. He was known for visiting folks in their camps scattered around town and giving rides to appointments, diapers for kids, financial assistance for those in crisis, and a prayer for everyone. I almost scrapped the plans for Relevant Hope because I didn't want to duplicate the services Barry was already offering.

In my first discussions with Barry, however, he shared that he really didn't go to camps much anymore since his time was focused on his meal services and his duties as an associate pastor at a nearby church. With his encouragement, we launched our work, but the name "Brother Barry" never stopped when we would visit folks. Some people thought we were from Barry's ministry because of the credibility he had in the community and the sad fact that no one else made a point to visit homeless camps consistently.

Barry never stopped serving in the community, and we often find ourselves working together. I've spoken at his services when he was out of town to speak at a conference. He has taken care of particular needs we couldn't meet for other people. He refers people to us who need a tent. We join him on Wednesdays to spend time with people and sometimes help serve soup or drinks at the park. We have the advantage of knowing we are in the kingdom business, not the business of competing with each other.

There is part of this story I haven't mentioned that is vitally important. Barry is a Methodist, I'm a Baptist, and Dillon comes from a Bible Church background. Our volunteer team also includes Presbyterians, Anglicans, those from the Assemblies of God, non-denominational folks, and many others. "Together We Can" applies first to the kingdom. We accept our distinctive differences, but we don't let these differences divide us or keep us from working together to serve those in need. We aren't out there to argue about predestination, mode of baptism, or the end times. We are there to demonstrate our love for God by loving people, serving their relevant needs, sharing with them the saving force of the gospel, and helping them transition from homelessness to a stable housing situation whenever possible.

We all work for the same High Priest and are building the same kingdom. I'm pretty sure there aren't going to be any "I told you so" bumper stickers in heaven. Together we will serve Christ, and together we will share the gospel to those in need of a Savior. There is no Methodist gospel, Baptist gospel, or Lutheran gospel. There is only one gospel. We have one gospel of Jesus Christ we all preach for the glory of God alone.

WHEN ATHEISTS SHOW UP TO HELP

Shortly after we incorporated Relevant Hope, another group of people were trying to figure out how to serve the homeless in their community. They came across a couple of news articles that mentioned us and gave me a call to ask if I would come to their meeting the following week to discuss the work we were doing and how they could help. I agreed and met them at an American Legion building in the small city of East Ridge, Tennessee.

I spent about half an hour explaining the work we were doing and how easy it would be for them to replicate the work or to join us. They decided that partnering with us was a great idea, and the East Ridge Homeless Coalition became Relevant Hope East Ridge.

Jamie, one of the volunteers we inherited from the group, was really curious about the religious nature of the work we were doing with the services we provided. I explained that we don't require participation in any kind of church service or religious program to receive our help. Our goal was to meet needs, including spiritual needs, as people desired. She then told me that she was a board member for the Chattanooga Freethought Association. Freethought groups welcome all freethinkers, atheists, agnostics, and skeptics.

Group members join together for fun and interesting conversation and to promote what they term "positive atheism through community service" as well as peaceful activism. ("Positive atheism" is intended to provide an alternative to the popular militant atheism and demonstrate that not all atheists are interested in attacking religion.) This made for an interesting situation in which an unbeliever was interested in joining a group of Christians to help the homeless.

Jamie was very interested in helping us with our work, and she wanted to get some other members of her freethought group to join the projects we were doing. I was probably more hesitant to bring them out with us than they were to work with us, but I trusted that God knew what He was doing, and I could trust that He brought Jamie to us for a reason.

Jamie called and asked for an opportunity to visit some of the camps. The first time we found a bunch of camps, but no one was home in any of them. Eventually we came across some people, and she did an awesome job interacting with each individual and never showed signs of uneasiness when we spoke about Jesus.

We then talked about other ways she and her freethought group could help with the work we were doing. I recommended they join us for a service project. We would take a Saturday morning and bring their group out to conduct a massive cleanup project of a homeless camp. I had suggested this project because a local property manager was evicting one of the camps where we were serving.

Jamie and her friends showed up on a cold November morning to help us clean the camp and then move the people living there to new locations. Two of the people were moving further down on the south end of town, one was moving just across the street to a different patch of woods, and one used it as an opportunity to take responsibility with his income and rented an extended stay hotel room a few blocks away.

When we arrived at the camp, Pam, a resident, came out to greet us. I wasn't sure how she would react or if Jamie wanted me to mention the volunteers were all atheists, so I just said that they weren't from a church. Pam wasn't content to let it go. She kept asking if they were from a local college or some other religious organization. I finally looked at her and said, "Pam, they aren't from a church, and they aren't even Christians. They are atheists from the Chattanooga Freethought Association."

She looked at me strangely for a moment and said, "Wait, you're not lying to me, are you?" Once she realized I was not making this story up, she ran over to Jamie and her crew shouting how happy she was that a bunch of atheists were there to help them. I gave Jamie an "I'm sorry" look, and she shrugged it off like it was no big deal. The funniest part of Pam's reaction was when one of her camp mates came out to greet us and she said, "You need to come out here and meet these people. They are atheists, and they're serious about it, too." At that point, everyone had a good laugh, and any apprehension was gone.

The crew worked hard all morning hauling debris to the Dumpster, bagging up garbage, breaking down tents and loading them into trucks, and packing up the residents' belongings. We helped get everyone moved into their new camps and set up all of their tents with tarps for adequate shelter. Before we left the camp after packing up the last load, I stood on a stack of pallets to get everyone's attention: "While I have you here, it would be a shame for me not to take advantage of this opportunity—" I paused for what I knew was coming, and I was right. Almost immediately, one of the atheists said something about me preaching, and another said something about Darwin.

I let them finish making their comments and taking their jabs (all in fun) and then gave them a surprise. I told them how thankful I was for their help and that we would be glad to serve together in the future for similar projects.

Since then, this freethought group has continued to help and support our work on many other occasions. Some of them have joined on other service projects, one of them who drives a cab has used it to help us transport people for free, and some help with our monthly trips to visit camps where residents keep pets, called Furry Friend Friday (FFF).

The first Friday of every month is Furry Friend Friday. On that day, we take a veterinarian, a technician, and a volunteer or animal control officer to visit all of the homeless camps in our area with pets. The pets receive vaccines, flea, tick, and worm treatment, some food, and a medical exam by the veterinarian. Also, if they need spay or neuter services, we arrange those procedures for them as well. All of this care is provided at no cost to the people who own the pets. Some members of the Chattanooga Freethought Association were instrumental in helping us make this arrangement. Jamie and her former roommate went with us to the animal center to meet with the director and discuss the details of how this kind of service would look.

LEARNING FROM THE FIRST CHRISTIANS

When we read in Acts about the early church, we often focus on the apostles' teaching, the fellowship, the breaking of bread, and prayer (Acts 2:42). We usually use the verses that follow as commentary for these elements of the early church. I have found, however, that readers often miss the end of that passage, which reads that these first Christians were "praising God and enjoying the favor of all the people. And the Lord added to their number daily those who were being saved" (v. 47). A few things in this passage are important to consider. First, they had favor with *all* the people. "All the people" includes the people in the community outside of the gathering of believers. In our day, then, "all the people" include atheists, agnostics, those who belong to other religions, and even those who are hateful toward Jesus and Christians.

We know the early church wasn't compromising the apostles' teaching at this time. So why did they have favor with all people? I think part of the answer is found in verse 45 that says, "They sold property and possessions to give to anyone who had need." The people in this first church sold their own property and possessions to help people who weren't even believers. They were looking out for the well-being of pagans, Jews, and possibly even atheists. As a result, they had favor with all people.

CONVICTIONS WITHOUT COMPROMISE

We don't have to compromise our beliefs to work with people who believe differently than we do. Working with people across denominational lines does not mean we have to change our doctrines and convictions that make us distinct. Nor do we have to compromise our doctrines for the pagan or the atheist to look at us with favor. Though no one from our local freethought group has come to faith in Christ, I have an open line of communication with the leadership of the largest atheist social group in our area. I've been able to sit down for a meal with many of them and discuss the arguments for God's existence and hear their reasons for rejecting God. The best part is that even after we had those conversations, we could still enjoy each other's company and continue to grow as friends even when the person did not become a Christian. Even as I write this chapter, I have stayed in contact with Jamie to confirm parts of this story and her permission to mention it. Why? Because we are friends.

THE COMMON GOOD IS GOOD FOR EVERYONE

"A Buddhist, an atheist, a Baptist, and a Pentecostal walked into a restaurant for lunch." It sounds like the opening of a joke, but I actually had this experience recently. Each person there that day came because they wanted to help people in our community.

Becky called me after reading an online article about the work we were doing in Chattanooga. She told me that she was the executive director of a ministry in town and thought we should meet to see if we could help each other in any way. We made an appointment to meet at her office. I showed up Monday morning to see the work that takes place with her organization, called the Episcopal Metropolitan Ministries of Chattanooga (known as Met-Min). They specialize in homeless prevention by providing financial support to people who are behind on their rent, unable to pay their power bill, or have another need that prevents them from having a stable housing situation.

One of the people who works for Becky has the job title of stability navigator. Her job is to help people navigate through the chaos of their situations and land with a stable conclusion. Almost every call I make to the Met-Min is to work with the stability navigator. We usually have a situation where someone has just transitioned from homeless to housed and needs assistance to make their new circumstances more stable. Sometimes we have someone who is on the brink of making that transition and needs some assistance obtaining an ID, birth certificate, social security card, or something else Met-Min can help them secure.

I met Eve during an annual event in Chattanooga called "Project Homeless Connect." This is an event we hold each year where all of the area service providers come together to make ourselves available for the day to the entire homeless population. Eve was there representing the Mental Health Cooperative. She came by our booth to introduce herself and ask about Relevant Hope. We explained our on-site service philosophy and gave her a brief presentation of our mission. She said we had a lot of things in common and should sit down to meet.

We met in her office one afternoon, and she began to tell me about the wide array of services offered at the Mental Health Cooperative. We discovered that we had a lot of overlap in the people we serve since they are a safety net provider, which means that people without insurance can come to them for help and not be turned away. She also told me how their case managers travel to the clients and provide services, and in some cases, provide transportation to the office for an appointment.

We support each other today by referring people to each other for specific services. We also help Mental Health Cooperative find homeless clients that are missing appointments or are late getting their prescriptions refilled. They assist us by providing mental health services to people in the homeless community who need a more relational approach to getting help than what is offered at other safety net facilities in our region.

These stories are only a few of many of God at work through our "Together We Can" approach. Atheists, Buddhists, Catholics, Protestants, and others are all ultimately people. We don't have to agree with the faith, politics, or policies of everyone with whom we work to help the poor. There is no verse in the Bible that says we can only help those in need with other people who completely agree with our beliefs.

Some evangelicals have argued with me on this point and have said, "Well, at least the Apostle Paul preached the gospel when he worked together with others," citing Philippians 1:18 to support their claim. They'll say atheists or Buddhists aren't preaching the gospel, so we can't work with them in any capacity.

Keep in mind that through engaging in relationships with these groups, I have the opportunity to share the gospel with those who willingly work with me for the good of others in this life. As I pray and build friendships, God can and does work to change the hearts of unbelievers to consider the good news of Jesus. This approach is not compromise; it is serving the common good and sharing Christ as we are able along the way.

PERSONAL IMPACT

A supervisor from another agency and a local pastor traveled with me one day to visit some homeless camps. We were on our third or fourth stop when the pastor was talking to the guy we were visiting about his resemblance to Phil Robertson from the popular *Duck Dynasty* television series. He then asked if he had heard the testimony of Phil Robertson. Our friend said, "No, but I do have Jeff's testimony up on the shelf." This "shelf" was the small area in between the concrete supports and the roadway of the bridge. Jeff is one of our on-site pastors who visits a couple of homeless camps every week to provide church services.

Our outside neighbor was referencing a small tract that Jeff made as an easy way to share his testimony and the gospel. On the front of the tract was Jeff's booking photo from when he had been arrested many years ago. The inside of the tract tells Jesus' story of redemption in Jeff's life.

After discussing Jeff for a few minutes, the pastor asked if he could pray for our friend before we left, and the offer was graciously accepted. The supervisor politely waited but did not seem to share the faith of the two men who prayed together. As I was driving her back to her car, however, that situation came up in conversation, and it was an opportunity for me to find out where she was in her spiritual life. She is a self-professed spiritual person who believes in a higher power that she calls "the universe." She has a pantheistic view, but she is at least willing to admit the existence of some kind of higher power. I used this as an opportunity to have a conversation about the God of the Bible.

I shared my story of growing up in a Bible Belt Christian home that was driven by moralism rather than a meaningful relationship with the living Jesus. My life later moved into a state of what I described as apathetic agnosticism, which basically meant that I didn't know if there was a God, and I didn't really care. Later, I started exploring religions to find any truth I could and found the evidence that led me to Jesus.

Though she did not change her mind at that moment, I was able to help her question her pantheism, and I demonstrated solid arguments for the existence of the God of the Bible. I shared with her the names of several books I read that were instrumental in helping me understand a theistic worldview. She asked me to send her those titles so she could read the books for herself.

This is only one example of how using outside help for kingdom-based work can open opportunities for the gospel to reach beyond the target audience of our ministry. Together we can reach our neighbor with the gospel. Together we can reach our community with the gospel. Together we can reach our nation with the gospel. Together we can reach our world with the gospel. Together we can!

Our challenge has led us to unexpected encounters and changed lives that are transforming today and for eternity. Who knows where God will take you as you choose both to believe and to live out God's Word in your life? Don't just read the Word; do what it says!

A FINAL WORD

JIMMY TURNER

We recently shared this story with our friends on social media:

> Last night Relevant Hope volunteers came across a mom and her two toddler-aged children in the woods who had nowhere to go after being forced out of the shelter where they were staying because one of the children has pink eye.
>
> We assisted this family by providing them somewhere to go for the weekend until the child's eye could clear and they could return to the shelter, but they need some help with a few items.
>
> One of the boys needs a new pair of shoes. The mom isn't sure what size he needs because of the width of his feet. They also need some extra baby wipes and are in desperate need of a stroller. The stroller they are currently using has a broken wheel that makes it difficult to control. Please contact us if you can help.

Within 24 hours we were able to provide a hotel room, shoes, baby wipes, and a stroller. It wasn't any one person but a movement of people committed to helping a family in need that changed the lives of a family at its point of greatest need.

Although we are unable to solve every problem, we help when and where we can. Each person is worth the effort. Each soul is an individual God loves and for whom Jesus died.

Since starting our work, we have focused on stories more than numbers. As of the moment we complete these words, however, we rejoice in one important number, the number 52. In less than two years, we have helped 52 people move from homelessness to housing. This number represents every visit, call, prayer, meal, and effort poured into the lives of the less fortunate. We want to share some of our recent success stories with you in this final section together.

CHANGED LIVES

When we first started working, we met Troy, who was very depressed and not sure how to continue. We poured into him with the love of Jesus, and he found the motivation to get back out and search for a job. We are happy to announce that he is working a full-time job again, and his boss offered to help him save half of his paycheck each week until he had enough saved to move back inside. He is now housed, holds a job, and contributes to the good of our community.

October 2013 was the first month we shared more than 1,000 meals in one month with the homeless in our community. This effort led to our work expanding from two to six homeless encampments. One of the people we met was a 65-year old woman named Pat who lived alone in the woods. We were able to move her tent into a more populated camp and she later became one of the first people we were able to see move from homelessness to housing.

That same month, one person we had been serving for several months named Joe moved in with family members. This housing arrangement started with the intent that he would help his mom and has since become a permanent location for him. He still comes to visit, but we don't expect to see much more of him in the camps.

In November 2013, we helped a man named Richard for months who later served time in jail. I continued to maintain contact with him, visited him in jail, and helped him make plans for when he was released. While incarcerated, he attended services and signed up for meetings to help support him through addiction. He was released December 1, and we were there to help.

That Christmas, our East Ridge volunteers prepared a huge meal to deliver to the homeless camps on Christmas day. The meal included two smoked hams, several casserole dishes, and deviled eggs. They also purchased new sleeping bags and thermal cups that they wrapped and distributed as Christmas gifts. One of the men had not received a wrapped gift in so long that he took five minutes to open it so he could savor the moment. Pete said, "You guys coming out here means more than you will even know. It is nice to not to be forgotten."

In January 2014, I went to check on the camps where I knew people had stayed during one of the coldest nights of the winter. When I came across Howie, he was naked from the waist down and had only a thin blanket wrapped around him. He was wet and cold to the point that he had ice crystals hanging from his beard. Howie had been caught in the rain the night before, and by the time he made it back to his camp, he found his tent flap was open and everything was wet except one blanket. That thin blanket and Howie's answered prayers are all that kept him alive that night until we found him the next morning.

When we found him, we immediately provided dry clothes, blankets, and a new coat. Later in the day, Howie gladly accepted when we offered to house him in a hotel room for a week. Howie made the most of his time in the hotel room. Instead of watching TV, he took the bus around town to apply for every available job opportunity he could find. Howie had a job before the week ended. With financial support from our ministry and friends from Met-Min, we were able to pay for Howie's room until he received his first full paycheck. We were also able to provide Howie with food and a 31-day unlimited bus pass that would provide him transportation to work and other appointments he needed to fulfill. Soon, Howie was helping us deliver food to others!

When Robert and his girlfriend, Ty, came to Chattanooga, they were already homeless. They moved to town for work and had been looking for jobs. When we first found them, they were living in a tent near an area of town called Camp Jordan. They suffered a couple of tragedies while living outside in our area but continued to work toward their goal of a stable life inside instead of letting their circumstances dictate their hope. We provided church services on a weekly basis in the camp where they lived. When it was extremely cold outside, we helped them get into a hotel room for a couple of weeks to find protection from the elements. Before long, they found out they were pregnant and expecting their first child. This news gave them added incentive to find help and improve their circumstances.

Our friend Will Wallace took reporter Josh Roe from News Channel 9 to visit Robert and Ty in connection with a story on homeless veterans and a new program available to help them. Shortly after the story aired, a gentleman called the station asking how he could get in touch with Robert to help. This gentleman had a doublewide trailer sitting on some property that he wanted to offer to Robert and Ty for housing.

I then connected Robert with the operations director for the new VA program to help homeless veterans, who was able to certify him into the program and offer funds to cover their living expenses for three month until they could pay their own expenses. Robert and Ty are now living inside, married, and have a beautiful child together.

In April 2014, we saw God work in the life of a man named Jack. Jack is a military veteran who lived in the woods outside of downtown Chattanooga. He previously lived with his brother and a friend in an extended stay hotel, but medical bills forced them to set up camp. When we met Jack, he had no idea what he was going to do but often said that he was willing to do whatever it took to get out of a tent. As we interacted with Jack on a weekly basis, we were able to connect with our friends in the Mission Accomplished Stable Housing (MASH) program that helps homeless veterans get into sustainable housing. Jack moved into a house and was able to leave behind his life in the woods. Since then, he has offered his extra bedroom to other homeless veterans while they wait for MASH to find them a sustainable housing situation.

In May 2014, the Chattanooga homeless community faced a devastating blow when a large tent community was bulldozed. Local citizens and friends of Relevant Hope shared the photos we posted to more than 13,000 people. Thankfully, the news was not all tragedy. With the help of donors and partner agencies, we were able to replace all of the tents that were destroyed and relocate every single one of the 30 people who lost their tents and possessions.

Brad became a friend of ours when he moved into a camp we served near Lookout Mountain. Brad is an Army veteran who suffers from heart attacks, strokes, and other terrible health conditions.

Brad's continued desire, however, was to have meaning and purpose in life. Brad came to faith in Jesus and was baptized at Morris Hill Baptist Church. He took responsibility with his disability and moved into an extended stay hotel to get off of the streets. Brad later moved to Washington to be with his son and live closer to his family members.

Keith lived in a tent in the local area for more than five years but was rarely noticed by anyone around his camp because he left at first light, didn't return until evening, and camouflaged his camp so no one could see it from the road. Keith worked for what he needed to survive, but he always enjoyed when we would come visit. Keith reconciled his relationship with his daughter and moved to Florida to enjoy a second chance with his family.

Bryant and Gena are two people who have an incredible tenacity for overcoming the odds. We met Bryant and Gena in 2013 when they needed a tent. Before they even received the tent, they volunteered with us to clean up a camp during a service project. They told us then that they weren't planning to stay homeless, and they were going to do whatever it took to get indoors and have a good life.

We were thrilled when they did just that. After four months of living on the streets, they were able to get jobs and work their way into an extended stay hotel. Soon, they obtained secure housing. We even helped them collect household items to make their apartment feel like home. We were glad to have been even a small part of their progress to housing.

In December 2014, we celebrated our friend Jennifer, who had lived in the homeless community for several years, hiding from an abusive relationship that cost her the custody of her children. Jennifer was one of the first people we began helping when we started Relevant Hope. She worked hard to reconcile her relationship with her family and prove that she was a responsible member of society. Jennifer has since been able to move back to her hometown, where she is working and able to see her children on a regular basis for the first time in years. We are proud of Jennifer and the changes that have taken place in her life.

In February 2015, tragedy struck Chattanooga's homeless community when one of our outside neighbors died from exposure to the elements. With local shelters at maximum capacity, we threw caution to the wind and focused on saving lives. As a result, we were able to help 41 people get into hotel rooms during the zero-degree weather and subsequent snow that followed. Our work literally saved lives, and some of these people are now dear friends we continue to help in other ways.

These stories are why we "do what it says." Not every story is successful, nor is every victory permanent. We have experienced far more unsuccessful stories, as well as criticisms from both our community and fellow Christians. What we do is not always safe, and it is rarely easy, but these transformations and others like them in the lives of the most vulnerable and neglected people in our communities are worth it. God created them for a purpose. He loves them so much that He gave His Son Jesus to die on their behalf. He calls us to show this same kind of love. We are not merely to read the Word and to deceive ourselves. When we "become the Bible" to those in need, God uses us in unexpected ways to change lives now and for eternity. Don't wait. Accept the challenge. Do what it says.

DISCUSSION GUIDE

The following discussion questions are designed to further your learning in either a personal or small group setting. Each set of questions includes five questions to help you reflect on key principles for action in your own life and community. These are not right or wrong questions but serve as starting points to encourage your application of biblical truth to help those in need.

In addition, you have the opportunity to use this material as an eight-week study for your church or other group. Additional ideas can be found at RelevantHope.org. If you would like to connect personally with the authors, please contact us at info@relevanthope .org. We would be happy to hear from you and possibly even connect with your group or check by phone, videoconference, or in person at a live event. May God bless you as you "do what it says!"

CHAPTER 1: DO YOU REALLY BELIEVE THE BIBLE?
Pretest on Faith and Action

1. What is the spiritual climate of your community? Would it be considered a culturally Christian area or not?

2. In what ways do you see a disconnect between the Christians in your community versus the social needs that exist? What do you see as some of the top social problems where you live?

3. What would it take to be known as a "friend of sinners" where you live? Name some actions you could start doing to show God's love to those often neglected by society.

4. Would you be convicted for being a Christian if it was a crime? What evidence would be used?

5. What are some ways you are or your church is practicing faith in action? What are some new areas you would like to pursue?

CHAPTER 2: A KINGDOM NOT OF THIS WORLD
Faith + Politics - Hatred = Impact

1. Why are Christians often fearful of engaging in politics or community service activities? What are the potential problems that could be involved?

2. What are some of the most important observations you see in the account of the Good Samaritan? How could these observations be applied to your life and community?

3. Do you feel like God has given you a dream or vision to help a particular group of people in your community? What is your dream? What are you doing to fulfill it?

4. What are some radical or bold ways your church could help those in need where you live? Green Street allows people without a home to camp on their church property and offers food and other assistance. What similar outreach could you or your church begin?

5. How can you both "work small and dream big" to help people in your community? What is one thing you could do today to start the process?

CHAPTER 3: TAKING SCRIPTURE SERIOUSLY
You Mean You Really Believe This Stuff?

1. When we talk about people being created "in God's image," what does this image mean? How should this belief change our thoughts and actions toward those around us?

2. What are some of the groups or types of people often neglected or mistreated in your community? In what ways could you show unconditional love to people in these situations?

3. Why is biblical love more than emotions? In what ways can 1 Corinthians 13 apply to serving those in need in your community?

4. When was a time that your attempt to help someone backfired, maybe in a similar way to Jimmy's story of setting up camp for John and Cathy? What are some of the ways God works even in these difficult situations?

5. How do Christians and churches often value education above application as a sign of spiritual maturity? What do you think would be a more helpful approach?

CHAPTER 4: TAG, YOU'RE CALLED
For Many Issues, You Already Know God's Will

1. When was a time you struggled to know God's will about an important decision? How did you feel? Why can discovering God's will be so frustrating sometimes?

2. What are some ways God has worked through your circumstances to reveal His plan for your life?

3. Why is it important to "start where you are" when attempting to discover God's will? What are some ways you can begin where you are today to find God's will for your life?

4. The woman who poured perfume on Jesus "did what she could." What are some ways you can do what you can today? If you removed every excuse for serving others, what could you do in the next hour to help someone else?

5. In what ways is endurance the key to fulfilling God's will? How can not enduring hurt the way we serve God and others?

CHAPTER 5: FOLLOWING THE GREAT COMMISSION *AND* THE GREAT COMMANDMENT
Jesus Didn't Say, "Choose One of the Above"

1. What are some of the ways the Great Commandment and the Great Commission are related? Why is it important *not* to separate these two commands?

2. Jimmy shares that "the napkin" became the key to evangelism in his life. What are some ways you could offer simple service that would impact someone who may not know Jesus?

3. What are some of your misconceptions about those who are homeless? Why do you think people have such stereotypes? What is the appropriate biblical perspective to have?

4. This chapter discusses that we are "saved to serve." How does the example of Jesus show us the importance of using our new life to help others?

5. Several stories of changed lives are shared in this chapter about the results of both showing love and making disciples. What are some stories in your own life in these areas? How have you been impacted by the service of others in your life?

CHAPTER 6: CTRL + ALT + DEL CHURCH
A Fresh Look at Church in Action

1. What are some of the things that come to mind when people talk about church or going to church? How are these often different from what is seen in New Testament churches?

2. Why is it important to discuss the fact that Jesus was sometimes homeless? How can this change the way we view and serve others in need?

3. When you read Jesus' words about the "least of these" in Matthew 25:40, what are some of the types of people in your community who come to mind? Who would be considered the least of these where you live? What could you do this week to serve some of them?

4. What would it look like to "get dirty" in serving others in your community? Consider some examples. Challenge yourself to try out one of these opportunities with a friend in the next few days.

5. How could your small group or church "be the church" in your community? What is one thing that would stand out in a major way toward helping those in need where you live?

CHAPTER 7: CONTROVERSIES 'R US
When Taking a Stand Means Taking a Hit

1. Have you ever been ridiculed or persecuted in some way for your beliefs? What happened? How did this experience make you feel?

2. In this chapter, Dillon writes, "If you're not being persecuted in some way, you're not doing it right." Do you agree or disagree with this statement? Why or why not?

3. Dillon notes, "Treat people like family because they are." How would this attitude change the way you treat the most vulnerable people in your community? What would you change immediately as a result?

4. Once in a while, an act of service overwhelms someone so much that they respond by saying, "I can't believe this is happening!" What kind of service would be required in your community to overwhelm others with love? Consider one option in this area and help make it a reality this week.

5. What would it mean to "be the news you wish to see in the world" in your community? Brainstorm some ideas in writing or with a group and choose something big to attempt where you live.

CHAPTER 8: TOGETHER WE CAN
Applying Scripture Is a Team Sport

1. What are some of the fears or concerns Christians have about serving with people from other groups? What are some of your personal concerns?

2. How would you respond if a group of atheists wanted to work with you to serve the poor in your community? In what ways could you work together for the common good?

3. Is there another Christian group or church in your community who would make a great partner in serving your community's needs? What would it take to coordinate your services better to help others? How could you personally help make this partnership happen?

4. What did you think when you read about Furry Friend Fridays? Did you think it was helpful or not? Why do you think homeless people

with pets and even those with no Christian faith would see this outreach as a positive form of help?

5. In what ways could you serve your community with another organization without compromising your beliefs? Consider one area where you would like to serve community needs and find a group that already works in this area. Contact them and see how you could do something together, even if it is only a one-time project.

APPENDIX: MINISTERING TO INDIVIDUALS WITH PTSD

———— JIMMY TURNER ————

Mental illness is a tragedy that is often misunderstood and wrongly shamed because of ignorance. When I was a kid, I was diagnosed with attention deficit hyperactivity disorder (ADHD). The doctor gave my parents a prescription that was supposed to help, but my father wasn't about to let me take medication for it. His remedy was more discipline, and he thought that I should learn to control myself better.

As an adult, doctors started to make similar suggestions to me about my kids. Originally, I thought I was supposed to follow in the footsteps of my upbringing. My wife, however, had enough sway and patience to convince me to give some real thought to mental illness and disorders.

I don't claim to be an expert on mental health, but being a person who is under treatment for mental health issues, having a son who falls into the autism spectrum with Asperger's Syndrome, and having a child who has ADHD, I have some experiences that a person can't find in a textbook. In addition, I work with people on a daily basis who suffer from a wide array of mental health issues that prevent them from enjoying a stable living condition.

Just recently I received a phone call from a man in the homeless community who was concerned because he was hearing voices. A year ago, another man called me from the parking lot of a restaurant to tell me his dead ex-girlfriend was standing in front of him and telling him to do things. We have still another friend who goes by two different names depending on who she is that day. Another person we work with may or may not recognize us when we come to visit him, even though we have seen him at least once a week for the last year and a half.

In recent years, our society has started to put a name on a mental illness that has plagued combat soldiers for years. It has been called *shell shock, soldier's heart, irritable heart,* and *battle fatigue.* Currently, medical professionals use the term posttraumatic stress disorder (PTSD). Whatever else PTSD is, it is important to remember that it affects more than just soldiers returning from war. Combat just happens to be the arena in which medical professionals have been able to leverage public attention about the widespread problem of PTSD and make it a mainstream issue.

One of the ladies we work with in the homeless community suffers from PTSD from a time when she witnessed a murder. Another woman in the community witnessed her father shoot her mother and grandfather while she hid under a bed. Additionally, a man in the homeless community experienced trauma in a marriage that led to PTSD. These stories are not to take away from the reality of PTSD for people who have experienced military combat, but we can't isolate this disorder to only people who have been exposed to war.

My PTSD wasn't diagnosed until after I was out of the Marine Corps. Many of my friends from the Marine Corps are suffering from this disorder every day, and at least one of the men from my unit killed himself by self-medicating with alcohol to treat a disorder that caused him shame.

Having PTSD doesn't mean that you were on the front lines of combat, either. Some people were deployed to war zones and never saw combat, but they did experience trauma that affected them through PTSD. For some people, their own actions triggered their PTSD, while others were traumatized by an event they experienced or witnessed. PTSD does not discriminate between men or women, ethnic backgrounds, or upbringings.

This section is not intended to provide you with any medical expertise on PTSD, but I want to share with you a little about it because it is something that affects me personally and the people we help in the homeless community. My PTSD is mild in comparison to others, but I've also been receiving treatment for several years. After I was diagnosed, I didn't seek treatment immediately, but much of what my wife and I experienced after I returned to the States made more sense. If my wife tried to come to bed after I was already asleep, she risked being hit, kicked, or thrown across the room. To avoid this, she would go to bed before me. We had to purchase a king-sized bed so we wouldn't touch each other at night. Otherwise, I would respond in my sleep the same as if she was coming to bed to attack me. When she wanted to wake me in the morning, she would stand at the door, turn on the light in the room, and say my name louder and louder until I would wake.

I exhibited what is called hypervigilance, which is where someone is always looking for a problem to happen. I had and still have an exaggerated startle reflex. At times, someone may try to sneak up on me, and if they startle me, I will react with much more exaggeration than most people, or I may not react at all. I never know how I will react in such a situation. I'm always uncomfortable in crowds. I can't explain what happens when I get into a crowded room, but it usually ends up with me in a corner or outside and angry without any good reason. I have trouble sitting in a room without my back to a wall, or at least the illusion that my back is to a wall, like in a high back booth or with a pillar behind me. I generally sit where I can see the doors in any room.

The treatments I've received have helped in many of these areas, but none of them have been a cure for some of what I endure as a result of my PTSD. Like I said before, my PTSD is mild compared to that of many others. At least my symptoms could be treated or mostly confined to my house. Our friends living on the streets who suffer with PTSD are constantly under the watchful eye of local law enforcement, business owners, and residents. They aren't merely paranoid that people are watching them; people really are watching them. Add something like hypervigilance, and you have a recipe for disaster, even without taking into account the many other symptoms and effects of PTSD. The homeless don't have a wall on which to rest their back or a door to watch. They rarely get to walk into a room that they can scan for threats because they are outside and everything is a threat.

It's no secret that a lot of people in the homeless community also deal with some kind of substance abuse or addiction. We've all seen the caricatures of the drunken bum holding a sign for more beer money. Sometimes this caricature is true, but sometimes that drunk is a person suffering from a mental disorder who doesn't even know who to call for help or how to find treatment that is available for him. His substance abuse is a feeble attempt to medicate his problems, because that man has experienced the unimaginable in his life.

Remember the woman I told you who witnessed a murder? She is a committed alcoholic because she doesn't get real treatment for her PTSD. The other woman who watched her dad shoot her mom and grandfather? She uses several different drugs to deal with the effects of her PTSD.

Not all substance abusers are self-medicating, but I'm not a medical expert, and neither are most of you reading this. It isn't my place to judge whether they are drunk because they have a mental disorder or for some other reason. It is our responsibility to show that person the love of Christ. That responsibility doesn't mean you have to support the person's addiction, but what if you kept a gift card to a fast food restaurant in your car, wallet, or purse to hand out? Maybe you could slow down your busy day and pull over to talk to someone on the street. Get to know him for a few minutes, and then come back to see him again later. Build a friendship with him that will help you better identify the relevant needs in his life. Then, you can apply some of our strategies to help him stabilize his life.

I didn't submit to treatment for PTSD until a doctor defeated me with logic one day in his office. I told him I was fine and could deal with it on my own. He asked me a question that changed everything for me. He said, "Jimmy, do you think a diabetic gets mad at his pancreas for not creating enough insulin?" I told him, "I don't suppose so." After all, a diabetic has no more control over how well his pancreas works than any other internal organ. He looked me square in the eyes and said, "And, neither do you have any more control over the way your brain has responded to the trauma you have experienced." I was floored. That was my "aha" moment.

Someone else out there is just waiting for his or her "aha" moment that will give them permission to get help. You may be the person God has placed in the life of another to help them through their trauma. This calling is not a problem to avoid but a ministry in which you can participate that can change the lives of those who have endured much pain.

FREQUENTLY ASKED QUESTIONS
ABOUT RELEVANT HOPE

1. Where did the idea for Relevant Hope originate?

I (Jimmy) went on a short-term missions trip to Miami in 2012. During that trip, I had the opportunity to work with some of Miami's homeless population. God used that experience to change the stereotypes and caricatures I had about homeless people. I realized that these were people made in the image of God and that they deserve the same level of dignity and respect as anyone else. When I returned to Chattanooga, I knew I wanted to help in the local homeless community. I volunteered and supported local agencies with my time and resources, but I noticed that all of the agencies providing services to the homeless had one thing in common: if someone wanted the help they had to offer, they had to come to them to get it.

As I read through Scripture, however, I was struck by Jesus' actions. He left heaven and emptied Himself of His divine glory to become a man. While He was physically present on earth, He didn't set up a program in the temple or a synagogue and offer Himself to anyone who would come to Him. Instead, He traveled to the streets and found the people who needed help. He touched the untouchables and sought the one in need.

Dillon was a professor for a couple of classes I was taking in college. We were speaking after class one day about my plans after college, and that is when I told him of my desire to provide on-site service to the homeless in Chattanooga. He shared with me his desire to do some kind of street church for the homeless, and we brought our two ideas together to form Relevant Hope.

2. What has been the reaction from other agencies that work with the homeless?

Chattanooga has a lot of great organizations that provide help to the homeless in our area. Since we've started, we've connected with many agencies and developed a strong partnership with them. One of the greatest parts of the relational approach we take to serve people is that we can rely on the agencies that take a programmatic approach to service in a positive way. We are in the business of helping people. In the nonprofit world, that means we can work together without competing against one another.

3. How do you find the homeless camps that you visit?

Finding homeless camps requires multiple strategies, patience, and community support. When we first started trying to find camps, we would search newspaper archives to see where known homeless camps were. This approach led us to many dead ends. I reached out to a former co-worker whose husband works as a police officer to ask for help. He shared with us about a couple of locations on the south end of town. We set out one Sunday morning around 7 a.m. and checked the places he recommended without finding anyone— until we reached our last stop. That is when we found Tree, who helped us find a camp that was only a few hundred yards away from his camp.

Later, we received more help from other people in the homeless community to find new camps, but that option wasn't a feasible one for finding all of the camps in our area. Dillon and I would look at satellite map pictures of different parts of town and then go scout those areas early in the morning or on his lunch breaks at work. We would target wooded areas, bridges, and railroads. Abandoned buildings were also great places to check for people living without a home. Other times, we would talk to local business people in areas where we knew there were high concentrations of homelessness. They would guide us to areas around their businesses to show us where people were coming and going, and we would go explore those areas to see if we could find anyone. After we established ourselves in the community, we would receive phone calls from other people in the homeless community asking if we would come and visit them. We've identified about 60 different locations around Chattanooga where people are or were camping. We visit each area as often as possible. We visit most areas weekly, but some of the areas where people have moved out or are transient in nature, we check at least monthly.

4. What seems to be the leading cause of homelessness?

The number one factor is broken families. The overwhelming majority of the people to whom we reach out have a breakdown in the family unit somewhere. Without a doubt, and with few exceptions, broken families are the leading cause of homelessness.

When I was discharged from the Marine Corps, I received my discharge papers and a moving truck. Because my discharge was medically based, I did not receive terminal leave, which meant I did not have the opportunity to leave my duty station early while finishing my accrued leave time, or anything else that would enable me to travel back to Chattanooga from Camp Lejeune to secure housing or a job. That fact meant that when I left base that day, I was, for all intents and purposes, homeless. My family had nowhere we could call home. Thankfully, we were able to stay with my mother-in-law. If we did not have family to support us for the couple of months it took to get a job and put back enough money to get a house, we would have been on the street or in a shelter, which is what happens in many cases.

People lose their job, house, and car, have no family available or no family relationships that will provide them with a place to stay, and they end up living on the streets. In other cases, people make poor life decisions that cause their family to send them away. We've come across people who haven't spoken to their family members for decades because they've been shut out of their lives due to drinking, drugs, or mental illness. We don't presume that we can tell those families they have to let these people come back into their lives, but some of our best success stories have been the direct result of restoring family relationships.

I've heard people who are homeless blame it on their drinking or drugs, or even claimed they choose to be homeless. The truth of the matter is that even the people who say they are homeless by choice would quickly accept housing if it were offered to them. Their choice is not to be homeless; their choice is to keep making the other choices they are making in life that will ensure their homelessness is sustained.

5. Isn't your work just making homelessness more comfortable?
Our first priority is survival. We can't help someone who is dead. There is an aspect of the work we do that requires us to provide resources that give people a sustainable quality of life to survive on the streets without every day having to be a fight for survival. On the other hand, we have found that when we are building relationships with people living on the streets, we develop a more meaningful relationship with them as friends instead of clients. We are then able to better identify the issues in their lives that either cause their homelessness or would prevent them from having a stable housing

situation. Having a closer relationship also means we can speak into their lives in a way others cannot. This relational strategy has translated into more people transitioning from homelessness to housed with less recidivism than other models that are based on getting people housed first and then providing case management to them.

We appreciate that those models are cheaper on taxpayers and are successful in many ways. Their success rate, however, is based on someone else providing a stable housing condition rather than them supplying it for themselves.

6. What does it look like when someone transitions from homelessness to housed?

This transition looks different for everyone. Some are able to get a job and will tolerate living out of a tent until they save enough to pay for utilities and move into a house or apartment. This situation is not the norm, but it does occasionally happen. Others get involved in a program that leads them into a housing situation through some kind of community home or public housing option. Veterans usually transition straight into a stable housing situation through one of the programs offered by the VA that give veterans a housing voucher.

When we are the primary facilitator of helping someone transition into housing, we try to help them first work through issues that would most likely cause them to end up back on the street. This strategy means that if they have some sort of mental illness or disability, we get them treatment. If they suffer from an addiction, we encourage them to go through a rehab facility. Once we deal with those issues, we want to find them a stable income. Sometimes that income is from some sort of disability benefit they are eligible to receive or through steady employment.

Since most jobs take a week or two before someone receives their first check, we pay for them to stay at an extended stay motel until they get their first check (upon verification of employment). We also provide them with a 31-day bus pass to ensure they have transportation to and from work. We will set them up with a week's worth of groceries and then take them to the food bank to help them get situated for their grocery needs. Once they get their first check, they will usually use it to stay in the extended stay hotel for a while because it is a cheaper alternative to paying rent, utilities, and a deposit right away. Most of the people we help spend a month or two in the hotel while they get used to being inside (living in a house/hotel/apartment). They can put back some money on their own or with our assistance and then transition from the hotel to a more permanent housing situation like a house or apartment.

7. What is the biggest misconception about homelessness?

One of the most common misconceptions I hear from people is that they are all just drunks or bums. I will often see videos on social media where people are shocked because they gave a person who is homeless some money, and they used it to buy food, get a hotel room, or help someone else. I see this sort of thing every day. Do some of them use it to purchase drugs and alcohol? Of course they do, but these are people who want to eat, take a shower, and help a friend just as much as anyone else. They are not primitive savages who mindlessly take money and think the only place they can spend it is in a liquor store.

God is going to judge us for what we did with the resources He gave us and not for what someone else did with the resources we gave them. God will judge them separately for their own actions. This observation, however, doesn't mean we should not be smart about how we provide for others. A simple solution is to carry five-dollar gift cards to common fast food restaurants in your car. When you see a person on the side of the road, hand them a gift card instead of cash. You'll be surprised how many will gladly accept it.

Another solution is to carry what we call "Hope Packs" in your car. It is a small drawstring backpack with some commonly needed items along with a five-dollar gift card (Contact us at relevanthope .org for an inventory list of what we provide in our Hope Packs). They are a great way to get small groups, school clubs, and social groups together to do something to help the homeless in an inexpensive but effective way.

8. What do we need to do to serve the homeless in our area better?

First, change your attitude about the homeless. They aren't homeless people; they are people who are homeless. No one identifies me as the white guy, or the SUV guy, or the student guy, and just the same, we should not identify people by their circumstances such as homelessness or poverty. I am an image bearer of God who is worthy of dignity and honor and respect. Every person has intrinsic value as an image bearer.

Do we believe the Bible enough to treat people like they are an image bearer of God, or are we too worried about another person's sin to see their intrinsic value? Jesus saw my sin and your sin and chose to die for us anyway because of the value He placed on us. I am in no better position to judge those around me than Jesus, so I'm going to continue treating them as image bearers and let God be the judge.

9. How many people are really homeless in the United States and in your local area?*

Many people seem to believe that the homeless can be stereotyped as the panhandler, the beggar, or the bum. In fact, homelessness does not seem to conform to any stereotype. It is true that many of the homeless do suffer from mental illness and addiction, but most do not. Most will never be seen or identified as homeless, and they should not be. Homelessness does not define them—it is simply a condition. The homeless among us are our neighbors, our co-workers, our family, and our friends. They are victims of circumstances that have resulted in a condition of homelessness.

The National Law Center on Homelessness and Poverty states that each year approximately 3.5 million unique individuals experience homelessness in America. Of that 3.5 million people, 25 percent are between the ages of 25 and 34 and 6 percent are aged 55 to 64. Children comprise 1.35 million, or 39 percent, of them, and 45 percent of the children are under the age of five.

According to the National Coalition for the Homeless (NCH), the primary causes of homelessness are poverty, eroding employment opportunity, lack of/decline in public assistance, and lack of affordable housing. The NCH identifies other contributing factors such as lack of affordable health care, domestic violence, mental illness, and addiction disorders.

The US Conference of Mayors reported that families with children are among the fastest growing segments of the national homeless population. Demographically, the national homeless population is estimated to be 42 percent African American, 39 percent white, 13 percent Hispanic, 4 percent Native American, and 2 percent Asian. Sixty-seven percent of the homeless individuals (not in families) are male, while 65 percent of those in families are female.

Of homeless adults, 30 percent are severely mentally ill, 18 percent are physically disabled, 17 percent are employed, 16 percent are victims of domestic violence, 13 percent are veterans, and 4 percent are HIV positive.

The US Conference of Mayors also determined that over half of all major cities cite domestic violence as a primary cause of homelessness among women.

According to information gathered for Chattanooga's *Blueprint to End Chronic Homelessness,* more than 4,094 individuals experience homelessness each year in Chattanooga, with more than 1,000 homeless children in public schools. Each night, an estimated 500 to 600 individuals sleep outside or in shelters with nearly 200 of them in families. Chattanooga reflects national trends when it comes to the rise in homelessness among families. Over the last several years, the number of homeless families has increased nearly 300 percent.

Each year, the Department of Housing and Urban Development's (HUD) Point In Time Count counts the number of homeless individuals on a given night in cities across America. It counts individuals living in shelters and on the street. The 2015 count found that 635 people were homeless in the Greater Chattanooga area.

Question 9 adapted and used by permission from the Chattanooga Community Kitchen at community-kitchen.org.

ABOUT RELEVANT HOPE

Known as the Scenic City, Chattanooga, Tennessee, has long been a vacation destination and thriving community of hard-working businesses, colleges, and churches. Unfortunately, many do not know the other side of Chattanooga's story. Despite tremendous economic and cultural development, deep societal problems continue to plague the area. One of the most demeaning has been the plight of the homeless.

Local statistics estimate more than 4,000 people in the Chattanooga area will be homeless at some point over the course of the year, with approximately one-fourth of these individuals being under the age of 18. On any given day, more than 600 people in our community live without shelter.

A popular "Tent City" consisting of homeless individuals was destroyed in 2010, communicating clearly that large populations of the unsheltered would not be allowed to remain visible to the public. As a result, many of these chronically homeless have disappeared into the shadows, sleeping in the forests of our community, in alleys, on street corners, in cars, under bridges, in parks, or anywhere they can find a place to rest.

More importantly, we believe God deeply loves each of these individuals because He created them in His image. In Luke 15, Jesus spoke of the importance of seeking the one lost individual over caring for the 99. Who will take the love of Christ to the "invisible people" of our community? Our country? Our world?

Beginning in 2013, Jimmy Turner and Dillon Burroughs began surveying homeless camps, talking with street people, and praying for opportunities to serve "the least of these" in their community. Relevant Hope was born, offering spiritual and humanitarian assistance to the homeless and poor of the community.

What is Relevant Hope? Relevant Hope is a complementary service to the many other homeless programs in Chattanooga. Instead of providing a static location from which to offer services to the homeless community, we go to the homeless camps that are scattered around town and provide services to them on-site. Through these efforts, Relevant Hope helps hundreds of people each week, with many moving from homeless to housed, unemployed to employed, and hopeless to hope-filled. Recent expansion has also begun to assist the homeless in Nashville and other locations throughout Tennessee. For more information or to find out how to serve the homeless where you live, visit us at RelevantHope.org.

ABOUT THE AUTHORS

DILLON BURROUGHS is a best-selling author and coauthor of more than 30 books on issues of spirituality and culture. Known for his collaborative efforts with faith-based leaders, his works range from editing *The Apologetics Study Bible for Students* to serving behind the scenes for some of today's *New York Times* best-selling authors.

In addition to writing and editing, Dillon is a frequent teacher, speaker, and commentator for a variety of outlets, teaching at some of today's leading Christian universities and speaking out against human trafficking. Dillon's works have been featured in more than 325 interviews, including appearances on Fox News, CNN, NPR, CBS, NBC, FOX, and ABC outlets, as well as leading Christian programs such as *Janet Parshall's America*, Kerby Anderson's *Point of View*, AFR, Moody Radio, and Way FM.

As a researcher, Dillon serves as senior writer at the *John Ankerberg Show*, a leading media ministry on presenting and defending the Christian worldview, broadcast weekly on television to more than 4 billion potential viewers in 200 nations and territories in several languages. He is also the primary writer for *The Ankerberg Minute*, a daily radio program broadcast on nearly 1,000 daily outlets in English and Spanish.

Dillon's writings include revising the bestselling "Facts On" series and "Comparing Christianity" series, through which more than 3.5 million people have been influenced regarding spiritual issues. In addition, his edited works have sold more than 4 million copies worldwide.

Dillon is the cofounder of Relevant Hope and currently serves as its executive director. He lives in Chattanooga, Tennessee, with his wife and best friend, Deborah, and their three children, Benjamin, Natalie, and Audrey. For more information about Dillon and Relevant Hope, visit DillonBurroughs.org and RelevantHope.org.

JIMMY TURNER is cofounder and former executive director of Relevant Hope. Numerous media outlets have featured Jimmy's efforts as a marine who now assists homeless veterans.

Jimmy's efforts recently gained recognition both locally and nationally. The Young Professional Association of Chattanooga nominated him as a finalist for the 2014 Civic Impact Award. The same year, he was also nominated for a CNN Hero Award for his work with homeless veterans. Chattanooga mayor Andy Berke also recently consulted with him on plans to end chronic veteran homelessness and reduce the city's homelessness by 80 percent.

In addition to his frontline efforts for the homeless of his own community, Jimmy writes for a variety of publications. Some of these publications have included articles for GotQuestions.org—the world's leading Christian question and answer website. He has also served as a contributing blogger for Activist Faith, a faith and action blog on Beliefnet.com, one of the nation's most popular spirituality web portals.

As a speaker, Jimmy is in demand at churches, conferences, and civic events where audiences are fascinated at his personal accounts of serving the homeless in times of crisis. Recent interviews with Jimmy include local Fox, NBC, CBS, and ABC affiliates, WAAK radio, Inspired Living Radio, and a featured article in Nooga.com. Irish reporter James Mahon also interviewed Jimmy as an expert for an upcoming documentary about homelessness in the southern United States.

Jimmy is a former adjunct faculty member of Tennessee Temple University and currently serves as the chief operating officer of Chattanooga Community Kitchen.

Jimmy lives in Chattanooga, Tennessee, with his wife, Shay, and their two sons, A. J. and Taylor. For more information about Jimmy and the Chattanooga Community Kitchen, visit Homeless Chattanooga.org.

TAKE YOUR FAITH JOURNEY ONE STEP FURTHER!

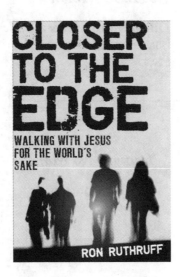

Closer to the Edge
Ron Ruthruff
ISBN 13: 978-1-59669-441-5
$14.99

How would the world's perception of Christians—therefore its perception of Christ—change if our way of doing justice work was as important as the end result? In *Closer to the Edge,* explore the heart of what it means to do justice, love mercy, and to walk humbly with your God in the world (Micah 6:8).

Also by Dillon Burroughs . . .

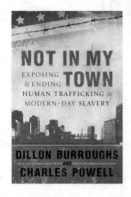

Not In My Town

Dillon Burroughs & Charles Powell
ISBN 13: 978-1-59669-301-2
$19.99

Hunger No More

Dillon Burroughs
ISBN 13: 978-1-59669-355-5
$12.99

Thirst No More

Dillon Burroughs
ISBN 13: 978-1-59669-312-8
$12.99

For information about our books and authors,
visit NewHopePublishers.com. Experience sample chapters,
videos, interviews and more!